© Alan Edwards

Planning and Periodisation

© **The National Coaching Foundation**, 2007

sports coach UK is the brand name of The National Coaching Foundation and has been since April 2001.

ISBN: 978-1-9055040-43-3

Author of this edition
Anne Pankhurst

Acknowledgements
With thanks to the following for their valuable input into this resource: Istvan Balyi; Sue Jolly, Graham Ross and Ian Stafford (all sports coach UK).

Coachwise editorial and design team: Christopher Stanners and Saima Nazir

Many of the ideas in this text are based on the concepts in *A Guide to Planning Coaching Programmes* © The National Coaching Foundation, 1998. Reprinted 1999 and 2003.

Authors
Bill Galvin and Paul Ledger

Sub-editors
Penny Crisfield, Phil Larder and Clare Palmer

Cover photo courtesy of Alan Edwards

Great Coaches...Great Sport

sports coach UK
114 Cardigan Road
Headingley
Leeds LS6 3BJ
Tel: 0113-274 4802 Fax: 0113-275 5019
Email: coaching@sportscoachuk.org
Website: www.sportscoachuk.org

Patron: HRH The Princess Royal

Published on behalf of **sports coach UK** by

Coachwise Business Solutions

Coachwise Business Solutions
Chelsea Close
Off Amberley Road
Armley
Leeds LS12 4HP
Tel: 0113-231 1310
Fax: 0113-231 9606
Email: enquiries@coachwisesolutions.co.uk
Website: www.coachwisesolutions.co.uk

Throughout this resource, the pronouns he, she, him, her and so on are interchangeable and intended to be inclusive of both males and females.

sports coach UK will ensure that it has professional and ethical values and that all its practices are inclusive and equitable.

070025

Preface

Quality coaching should ensure improved performance, the realisation of potential and the opportunity for teams and individual performers to reach their goals. Good coaches ensure that the process of planning gives every performer the best chance of using their training to achieve success in competition.

Many different factors contribute to sports performance and the realisation of potential. The integrated development of the physical, technical, tactical and mental factors of performance (the Performance Factors) should lead to peak performance in the competitive environment. In team sports, teamwork will also need to be developed. The long-term well-being of performers is important when preparing for the competitive environment, so lifestyle factors such as education, the support of family and friends, careers, work, finances and health need to be included in any plan. Systematic planning methods for the long-term, medium-term or short-term development of performers are the only way that coaches and performers can manage and integrate all these issues efficiently and effectively.

This resource is for coaches who would like to develop and progress their planning skills for the development of their performers, whether that is for a lifetime in sport, for a four-year period, for a year or for individual sessions that are part of a longer-term programme.

A significant influence on the thinking regarding the long-term progressive development of young performers in the UK in recent years has been the Long-term Athlete Development model (LTAD). In essence, the understanding of the impact of growth, development and maturation on the training of young performers has significantly influenced many governing bodies of sport. LTAD is, in itself, a developmental plan and, therefore, underpins the planning and coaching process for young performers in many sports in the UK.

This resource is divided into two parts:

- Part A will help you to consider what information you need to obtain and think about in order to plan well.
- Part B will help you to bring all the information together in order to help you write different plans – for example, an LTAD programme for your sport, a plan to prepare performers for major events, such as the Olympics, an annual periodisation plan for an individual performer or team and, lastly, session plans that enable you to work with performers during different phases of the year.

Thus, the information in this resource moves from the 'bigger picture' to the detail of each session. It also progresses from considering each factor in isolation to the reality for coaches – the integration of all the different elements of performance, training, lifestyle and competition into a coherent plan.

The activities are intended to help you to apply your skills and knowledge to planning in your own sport and with performers for whom you have responsibility. Once you have worked through the information, you should be able to:

- understand the important contribution that quality planning makes to the development of performers in your sport
- understand the links between different programmes, individual and team development and planning in your sport
- generate information on your sport, the individual performer and/or the team to assist your planning
- integrate all the Performance Factors, their components, lifestyle and competition into individual and team training programmes
- understand the implications of LTAD
- understand, explain and apply the training principles and the adaptation process
- plan quadrennial, annual and session plans
- periodise the year into preparation, competition and rest/recovery phases
- design quality training programmes to meet the lifestyle needs of your performers
- adjust plans when unexpected events occur
- identify appropriate ways to assess and monitor performance
- identify areas where you may require further information or personal development.

Contents

Part A

Part B

Section 6 – Planning Models

Section 7 – Reviewing and Monitoring Progress

Glossary

Appendix A – Planning Tools

Appendix B – Assessment Tools

Appendix C – Performer Record Sheets

Part A
Section 1
Introduction

1.0 What this Section is About

This section provides an introduction to planning, explains what it entails and why it is important for all sports coaches. It also shows how an understanding of growth, development and maturation in young people underpins the principles of Long-term Athlete Development (LTAD). In a number of sports in the UK, LTAD is an important component of planning for young performers.

By the end of this section, you should be able to:

- describe planning models
- explain the components of planning
- explain the importance of planning to performance and the development of potential performers in your sport
- assess your current knowledge and abilities in the field of planning.

1.1 What is Planning?

The components of planning

In simple terms, planning involves considering all the aspects of performance improvement, and then developing a programme that takes performers and teams from where they are now to where they want to be. For performers to achieve their dreams, the planning and delivery of quality programmes cannot be a random process. It must be a systematic process, based on fact and the performer.

There are a number of components of the planning process:
1. **Knowing where your performers are now.**
2. **Knowing where your performers want/need to be.**

3. **Knowing the timescale** that will be necessary to move from where your performers are now to where they want and need to be. That time could be as long as four years (the Olympic cycle); it could be a year, two or three months, a week or even just a single session. In each of these timescales, the performers begin with certain skills and abilities and should finish with them at a higher level.

4. **Understanding your knowledge base as a coach** and knowing what needs to be done to take the performers to where they want to be in a set period of time. This means knowing your sport, your own performer or team and the opposition very, very well and also understanding the process of growth, development and maturation if you are coaching young performers.

5. **Knowing how to prepare the plans** – having accurate and relevant information on which to base your training programmes.

6. **Monitoring and evaluating the plans** – making sure that the plan stays relevant to the performer/team.

The planning process is a systematic one that integrates each of these issues.

Knowing where your performers are now

↓

Knowing where your performers want/need to be

↓

Knowing the timescale

↓

Understanding your knowledge base as a coach

↓

Knowing how to prepare the plans

↓

Monitoring and evaluating the plans

Figure 1: The planning process

Knowing where your performers are now

Quality planning depends on knowing where you want to go, but, to do that, you must have a clear idea of where you are starting from. As a coach, you must be realistic about the present skills, abilities and potential, *together with the motivation and commitment* of the performer/team, in order that you start from the right place. You also need to know a great deal about your performers, in terms of their lifestyles and how they manage themselves. Performers will have *dream goals*, but you will need to be certain of two things – that they have a realistic commitment to training and that you are able to create a motivational and challenging environment. Section 2 will help you with this.

Knowing where your performers want/need to be

It is important to clarify the performer or team's *dream goal*, as it will:

• shape the entire planning process

• provide a focus for the plan

• ensure commitment from both performer and coach

• ensure a common purpose for everyone.

The goal, however, will probably seem unattainable, unless it is broken down into smaller, more achievable steps. Thus, goal setting will provide information for your training programmes. Section 3 will help you with your goal-setting skills.

Knowing the timescale

Having identified the gap between the performer's/team's aspirations and their current abilities, plans must be designed and implemented that will take them from where they are now to where they want/need to be. Timescales for this will vary, but need to be realistic. All the components that contribute to successful performance must be included. If the plan is for a 10-year period, four years or for one year, then there will be different levels of detail for training and competition within each of these. The plan may be short term – one or two months or even a few sessions – and not include competition at all, in which case the level of detail could be high. The important issue to understand is that in developing performers, every session contributes to the 'big picture' and is therefore important. There are key skills in planning programmes and sessions and these are covered in Section 6.

© www.actionplus.co.uk

Understanding your knowledge base as a coach

It is not difficult to understand that to plan realistic and effective programmes for performers in a particular sport, the coach must have a real understanding and knowledge of:

• the sport itself, in terms of the skills and abilities needed by performers to excel (these will be different for each sport, although, clearly, there will be some commonalities)

• the performers themselves and also the lifestyle they have

• how to motivate performers and create a challenging environment for training

• the particular aspects of the sport – times/distances of successful performers, rules and regulations, etc

• the guidelines for LTAD-specific stages of development in the sport.

Knowing how to prepare the plans

There are important planning tools which are helpful in the process of preparing plans. For example, LTAD gives very clear guidance on the growth and development of young performers and indicates the Windows of Trainability (Opportunity) for different ages and levels of maturation. Clearly, to ignore such information in the planning process for young performers would not be sensible. Other techniques for performer assessment, such as goal setting and performance profiling, will probably be familiar to you. In Sections 2 and 3, you will use them to help develop your overall understanding of planning. If you feel you need further help in these areas, you will be referred to other sources, where the topics are covered in more detail.

Monitoring and evaluating the plans

Any plan is of limited value, unless it is monitored and evaluated. Monitoring is the process of recording information that will inform coaches and performers about progress (or lack of it) towards the performer's/team's goals. Evaluation, too, involves both coaches and performers making judgements on progress through the programme, and deciding whether or not amendments are necessary. Section 7 will help you to decide how you could monitor and evaluate your programme.

1.2 Why Plan?

For performers, achieving 'dream' goals means that they have achieved in their sport. They are performing at the peak of their ability. To reach this peak, the Performance Factors (physical, mental, technical and tactical) must be at an optimal level and be integrated with each other. It is the coach's task to ensure that the performer's programme of preparation for achievement includes all the components, and that each one is optimised by the performer at the right time.

It is important to remember that the Performance Factors cannot be developed in isolation, but build on, and are supported by, each other. The physical component of power, for example, may only be developed when the appropriate levels of strength and speed have been achieved. Power training may be enhanced by previous training in areas such as flexibility. Training effects are cumulative – blocks are built on previously laid blocks. These building blocks make complex structures and a coach needs sound planning skills to ensure the structures are well founded and integrated.

An understanding of growth and development shows us that, when working with young performers, there will be a number of components which can be developed rapidly at specific times. For example, the development of motor skills can be very rapid between the ages of eight and 12, whereas the development of strength comes towards the end of puberty. The Windows of Trainability (Opportunity) principle means that coaches should plan to work on specific elements of performance at the times when progress is likely to be fastest. In the example above concerning the development of power, it is unlikely that the young performer who has not yet reached physical maturity will be able to use this component to its greatest extent for some time.

In some sports, coaches must make decisions about the priorities for different Performance Factors – rugby players cannot devote all their time and effort to becoming stronger, at the expense of their endurance. Similarly, the multi-event performer cannot afford to improve at one event, but deteriorate in the others. Only detailed planning can ensure the correct decisions are made on training content and balance.

So, while knowing that different Performance Factors can be trained is a prime reason to plan, the coach should also know the **optimum** times to develop some skills in young performers and also be able to 'juggle' these to fit the different requirements of the sport.

1.3 Planning and the Coaching Process

It should now be clear that successful coaching is dependent upon coaches understanding planning at all levels. Planning is the framework for the entire process of preparation for performance, whether for a 10-year period or a single session. Therefore, the **coaching process should follow the planning process**, rather than the reverse.

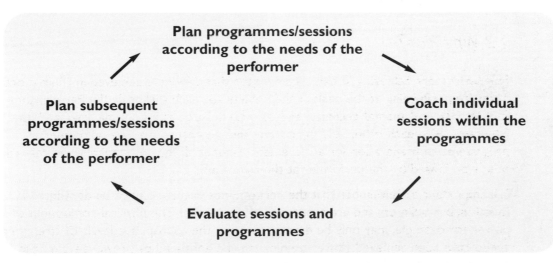

Figure 2: The coaching process

Planning must also recognise that coaching programmes need to be flexible because, in reality, a number of different events can occur that affect any plan. These can be personal matters, facilities or weather problems or reactions of the performer mentally and physically to a given training load. For that reason, longer-term planning must always enable the coach and the performers to adapt the training and competitive schedules in response to unpredictable events. Section 5 will help you to design balanced programmes of training and competition that take a holistic approach to a performer's development.

Planning for teams

In team sports, planning must occur at two levels:

• Individuals will have their own training programmes, to meet individual and positional needs. In the non-competitive phase of the year, individuals will follow their own individual training programmes almost exclusively.

• The team will have a programme of preparation that aims to produce an efficient and competitive unit that can achieve the goals of the team, as well as of each individual. During the competitive phase of the year, the team will train as a unit at every available opportunity.

© Alan Edwards

Both programmes, of necessity, must overlap and complement each other to an extent that varies according to the season. The performance of the team is dependent on the performance of the individuals within it. The challenge for the coach is to balance the needs of the individual with the needs of the team. Detailed planning is the key. Coaches who work with teams will need to develop a knowledge and understanding of each performer and then develop both individual and team programmes.

1.4 Planning Models

We have already discussed the idea that the planning of programmes can be placed in a number of different timescales, varying from a lifetime to a single session. Coaches working with elite Olympic performers are likely to plan for quadrennial and annual timescales, whereas coaches with younger and/or less experienced performers could use both a sport-specific LTAD framework for the long-term planning and detailed short-term programmes.

Clearly, the detail of planning at each level will vary and the single lesson is likely to have the most detail – exactly what will be trained, for how long and what the intended outcomes will be. But each level of planning **must** contribute to the 'big picture' and the achievement by the performer or team of the dream goals that they each hold. Each level of planning is discussed in more detail in Section 6.

Long-term plans

We have already referred to the Long-term Athlete Development model. In many senses, LTAD is probably the ultimate plan, since it maps out a lifetime's involvement in sport. Most coaches, however, will work within the 10–12-year 'rule' for performer development cited by Istvan Balyi, based on work by Ericsson in his research on expert performance, and familiar to many coaches from personal experience. From a number of standpoints, it is commonly accepted that the development of expert performance takes at least 10–12 years. LTAD demonstrates how the 10–12-year time frame is linked to the increasing maturity – growth and development – of young performers, beginning around 6–8 years of age. LTAD therefore is *a long-term plan*, structured to take account of the skills and abilities of the developing performer, in both chronological and developmental (biological) ages. LTAD has a number of key components that help us with the shorter-term plans that must underpin performer development:

- The ratio of training to competition is identified for each age and stage. This means that, as a coach, you can build the right amount of training and competition time for different ages into your programmes. In British sport, young performers often spend so much time competing (seeming to concentrate on short-term success) that they miss out on training the important skills and abilities that will help them to realise their potential in the long term and possibly on the world stage.

- The recognition that different ages and stages have different 'requirements' – in terms of the emphasis on the mental/emotional, physical, technical and tactical factors of performance – is important:

  - Young children who are beginning to take part in sport need to learn FUNdamental movement skills.

  - The emerging performer of 10–13 years of age learns to train and build on the FUNdamentals, for future competition.

  - In the years of puberty, learning to compete becomes the key issue.

  - For the realisation of potential, winning becomes the emphasis in early adulthood.

  - To remain in sport and have an active life, the performer trains and competes at a different level in the retaining stage.

- The recognition that certain sports require an earlier age at which specialisation in that sport should commence – gymnastics, for example, is an 'early specialisation' sport, while tennis and rugby are considered to be 'late specialisation' sports. These distinctions are important in the planning process and different examples will be given in Section 6.

- The Windows of Trainability (Opportunity) principle means that coaches know what is important to plan for and train at specific ages and stages.

- The difference between chronological age and developmental (biological) age is also crucial for coaches to understand and build into the planning process.

There are an increasing number of resources on the use of the principles of LTAD available and some of these are listed at the end of this section.

© Alan Edwards

Planning in four-year periods

Those coaches who are involved in Olympic sports are familiar with the four-year (quadrennial) cycle of planning, where the goal for training and competition is to achieve at the Olympic Games. By its very nature, planning such a programme for Olympic achievement requires, at least in the first 1–3 years, a more general plan, as well as a series of annual plans. Clearly, there are intermediate goals built into the annual plans along the way, but all of these are building towards the final objective of Olympic competition. These plans will be progressive throughout the four-year timescale, but the ultimate objective remains the same.

© Action Images

Annual planning

Annual planning is obviously a more specific level of planning, if only because the timescale is becoming more manageable. However, even in this timescale, the year will be split into different phases – typically preparation, competition and rest/recovery. The preparation phase itself is usually broken down into a general and then a specific phase, as the competitive phase gets closer. You probably know that this phasing of the year is known as **periodisation**. The length and number of these phases will vary from sport to sport, depending on whether the sport is seasonal or year-round. In a year-round sport, the different phases may be repeated two, three or four times (double, triple or quadruple periodisation), while in a seasonal sport, the plan will need to be constructed to ensure top performance through the (long) single competitive phase.

Periodisation also has cycles that help the planning process:

• A macrocycle is what its name suggests – this cycle includes all four phases in it, so, in a sport with double periodisation, there will be two macrocycles.

• A mesocycle is usually a period of 1–6 weeks within any phase of the plan.

• A microcycle is usually a training period of 2–7 days – thus, several microcycles are included in a mesocycle.

Session planning

The most detailed level of planning is the single session. As with every other level of planning, there should be specific goals for the session and one particular session should always be linked both to the previous and to the following one. In other words, single sessions are simply the *delivery unit* for every level of planning. In a single session, the coach can get down to the real 'nuts and bolts' of coaching and performer improvement so that, when put together with hundreds of other sessions, the performer or team can attain the 'dream goal'.

Activity 1

The following activity will help you to clarify the advantages of planning, and help you to understand some of the pitfalls that some coaches discover as they work through the process.

1. Read the following scenarios.

Scenario 1

Jenny is a swimming coach who plans every session and every training cycle thoroughly. She is responsible for the training programmes for all the swimmers in a regional squad from the ages of 12 to 21. She sits down with each swimmer, the swimmer's family, a psychologist and any other relevant people to plan the programme at annual and four-yearly intervals. In this way, she attempts to take account of each and every variable that might affect performance. Every month, she has a review and evaluation session with each swimmer. At this session, they will set goals for the following month and plan the monthly programme. Weekly planning sessions set the goals and content for each microcycle. After every training session, she reflects on the session with the swimmer and assesses whether the goals have been achieved. She then sets goals for the following session. The training programme evolves through the year and all goals are set as incremental improvements on the previous ones, in line with an overall target. Goals are mostly achieved. If it appears that a goal will not be achieved, the reason for it is thoroughly analysed and an adjusted goal set.

Scenario 2

Pete is an experienced rugby coach, working with a club under-15 squad. The number of matches each player in the squad plays in a season is planned. Pete decides on the content for each session with the players when they arrive at the ground. The performance of the team in the previous weekend's match determines the content of the session. They work on the aspects of performance that were not up to standard. Pete also believes that players must be enthusiastic about their training. If they want to work on a particular component, Pete will usually let them, provided that it is appropriate for their age and level of maturity. He believes it is most important that players have an input into and enjoy the sessions. In the run-up to important matches, however, Pete is more prescriptive with the players, ensuring that their training is at competition intensity. He also takes an interest in their school schedule and knows who plays school matches, as he believes that sufficient recovery is crucial at this age.

Scenario 3

Geeta is a triathlon coach. She is very experienced and knows exactly what it takes to achieve success. She is able to outline the precise content of each session that her performers will undergo in one month, or even six months, from today. Planning is the key to her success as a coach. Long-term, medium-term and short-term goals are planned for each macro, meso and microcycle (see page 8 if you are unsure of this terminology) from the beginning of the year. If performers are not meeting their goals, she pushes them harder to complete the required training. If they do not meet the required standards, they are better to stay out of her way! Discipline and hard work are the two key qualities required for success in triathlon. The performance standards are set by the opposition, so, in Geeta's view, the standards for performance at a certain level are not open to negotiation.

2. Based on these scenarios and your own experience, list some advantages of using some kind of formal planning process to direct your preparation for competition.

3. Describe the issues that you think arise from the scenarios above in planning for junior performers.

4. What steps do you think could be taken in the planning phase to avoid or minimise potential pitfalls in the delivery of the programme?

Now turn over.

1. Planning the performer's and/or team's programme will ensure that the coach:

- *includes all the factors that contribute to high-quality performance by the performer or team*
- *takes into account the issues that are key to coaching young performers*
- *prioritises the performance components on the basis of the performer's/team's strengths and weaknesses, and the time of year*
- *balances the time spent on the different Performance Factors and ensures that young performers develop the right skills at the right time*
- *ensures that training of different Performance Factors is complementary*
- *can build appropriately on previous gains*
- *has the opportunity and the criteria with which to review and evaluate the programme and measure progress of his/her performers/team*
- *is able to use the planning process as a motivational tool with performers*
- *is able to determine his/her own coaching effectiveness.*

2. The advantages of using some kind of formal planning process to direct your preparation for competition include:

- *Thorough planning can help create confidence in performers, especially if they have been involved in the process and if they know that their preparation has been as complete as possible.*
- *Careful planning should result in a familiar and practised preparation for competition. This can minimise the pre-event anxiety that may cause problems for some performers.*

And perhaps most importantly:

- *If not managed properly, planning can be a very time-consuming process that results in an inflexible approach, taking no account of individual differences.*

3. Planning for young performers must take account of a number of additional factors:

- *the age and stage of the performers, in terms of their growth and maturity*
- *the amount of competition in a year or phase*
- *the amount of physical activity being undertaken at school, in addition to club training. Potentially talented young performers are likely to be involved in several school sports, so good communication needs to be established with and between performers, parents, teachers and coaches.*

4. Any pitfalls in the programme could be avoided by:

- *planning step by step, but being very aware of the 'big picture' and how things need to fit together*
- *adopting a flexible approach and being ready to make adjustments to the programme*
- *making planning a normal part of training and competition.*

1.5 Where are You Now? Reflect on Your Current Planning Practice

Consider the following quote from Jurgen Gröbler, the gold-medal rowing coach, when referring to the Atlanta Olympics[1]:

> The standard and quality of competition was exactly as I had expected and my training schedules had been geared to the performance standards that I predicted would win medals. As a coach, you must know exactly what is going on in your sport in order to stay on top. Training in the Olympic year always requires the highest volume of training, although this must be monitored carefully. Regular physiological assessments and performance tests allow you to modify training loads as appropriate, as well as providing a consistent measure of improvement.

This quote may help you to place the planning process in a practical context. Now, you should consider how you already use planning in your present coaching. The following exercise will help you. Some of the information the exercise generates will be used in Section 4.

Activity 2

Give some thought to the following questions. Try to answer them honestly. Rate your ability from one to four, where one indicates poor knowledge or ability in the area and four indicates competence and confidence in the area. An understanding of the terminology used may also indicate your knowledge base.

(i) Can you outline the requirements for success in your sport, at the level of your performer or team?

    1   2   3   4

(ii) Are you able to assess your performers/team objectively against these requirements?

    1   2   3   4

(iii) How well do you understand the process of developing each requirement of your sport in individual performers?

    1   2   3   4

(iv) Do you divide the training year into phases which allow you to concentrate on different Performance Factors?

    1   2   3   4

(v) Do you know why and how to manipulate the training load in the various training cycles?

    1   2   3   4

(vi) Are you satisfied that your performers peak at the right time and for the right occasions?

    1   2   3   4

(vii) Can you explain the physiological and psychological bases for peaking?

    1   2   3   4

---

[1] Coaching Focus No 34, Spring 1997: Lessons from the Games. Leeds, National Coaching Foundation.

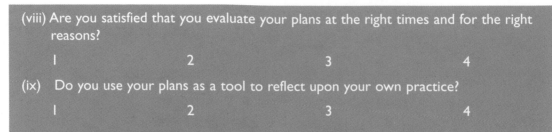

(viii) Are you satisfied that you evaluate your plans at the right times and for the right reasons?

      1   2   3   4

(ix) Do you use your plans as a tool to reflect upon your own practice?

      1   2   3   4

Now, review your answers. Identify the aspects of planning programmes in which you feel less confident (this means you will have scored yourself at 1 or 2 in the questions above):

Ask yourself why you do not feel confident in these areas. Is it a lack of knowledge or have you been unable to apply your knowledge to your present needs? Maybe you simply have not had time to think the problems through. Jot down the reasons for your lack of confidence in each of the areas you listed above.

In the space below, outline some goals that you would like to achieve by the end of studying this resource. These goals should be related to the areas identified above as your weaker areas.

These goals should provide you with a framework for your study. However, you may find that you benefit equally from those sections which provide a refresher course in the areas where you believe you are strong.

1.6 Recap and What Next?

This section has:
• explained what planning is
• outlined the reasons for, and levels of, planning
• explained that the planning process is an integral part of coaching.

You should now:
• have an overview of the planning process
• be beginning to think about how you use planning in your coaching at present.

This reflection is central to your understanding. It will help to make the content of the resource immediate and relevant so that the information will have a direct influence on your coaching.

In the following sections, you will learn more about the planning process; by examining each constituent part, you will be able to identify the format and procedures that best suit your sport and coaching style.

Bibliography

Ericsson, K.A., Krampe, R.T. and Tesche-Romer, C. (1993) 'The role of deliberate practice in the acquisition of expert performance', *Psychological Review* 100: 363–406.

Further reading

Balyi, I. (2001) 'Sport system building and long-term athlete development in British Columbia'. Canada: Sportsmed BC.

Ericsson, K.A. (2006) 'The influence of experience and deliberate practice in the acquisition of expert performance', in Ericsson, K.A, Charness, N., Feltovich, P. and Hoffman, R. (eds) *The Cambridge Handbook of Expertise and Expert Performance*. Cambridge: Cambridge University Press. ISBN: 978-0-521600-81-1. pp. 685–705.

Stafford, I. and Balyi, I. (2005) *Coaching for Long-term Athlete Development*. Leeds: Coachwise Business Solutions/National Coaching Foundation. ISBN: 978-1-902523-70-9.

Lee, M. (ed) (1993) *Coaching Children in Sport: Principles and Practice*. London: E and FN Spon. ISBN: 978-0-419182-50-4.

Lyle, J. (2002) *Sports Coaching Concepts: A Framework for Coaches' Behaviour*. London: Routledge. ISBN: 978-0415261-58-6.

Malina R.M., Bouchard, C. and Bar-Or, O. (2004) *Growth, Maturation and Physical Activity* Second Edition. Champaign, Illinois: Human Kinetics. ISBN: 978-0-880118882-8.

Starkes, J.L. and Ericsson, K.A. (eds) (2003) *Expert Performance in Sport*. Champaign, Illinois: Human Kinetics. ISBN: 978-0-736041-52-2.

Section 2

Information About Your Sport

2.0 What this Section is About

In order to plan programmes of training and competition at any level, as a coach, you will need information on a number of key issues:

1. Information about your sport

This section will help you to identify the information you need and give you details on preparing plans and programmes for your performers from the standpoint of the needs of the sport.

There are two other key areas of information you need to prepare high-quality plans for your performers and/or teams. They are:

2. Information about your performer and/or team

3. Information about goal setting – what the performer or the team want to achieve in a given period of time

However, both of these issues will be covered in Section 3.

In this section, the information that you gather about your sport will ensure your coaching is effective and focused.

By the end of this section, you should be able to:

• identify the specific role of each of the Performance Factors in your sport

• describe and analyse these factors and their components

• determine the optimal methods of assessing the current performer/team skills, fitness and potential skills and abilities in each of the components.

2.1 The Performance Factors

The starting point for developing any coaching programme is determining the demands of the sport itself. Every sport has the same factors, but the relative importance of them will be different:

- *Physical* (eg flexibility, speed, power, endurance)
- *Technical* (eg the motor skills needed to take part – kicking, striking, throwing, running, jumping, etc)
- *Tactical* (eg anticipation, knowledge of opponents, tactical and strategic planning, decision making)
- *Mental* (eg concentration, commitment, anxiety control).

The relative importance of the Performance Factors

Each sport will have different levels of demand in each of the Performance Factors, but training in each one is vital to the overall development of the performer. Therefore, all four will need to be built into your training plans.

Coaches must know the specific demands of their sport and be able to identify the relative importance of each factor. For example, a marathon runner's coach would probably rate the Performance Factors in the following order of importance:

    1 Physical   2 Mental   3 Tactical   4 Technical.

The coach of a club rugby team, because of previous experience and perceptions, might give the order of priority as:

    1 Technical   2 Tactical   3 Physical   4 Mental.

You might get different answers from different coaches within the same sport, perhaps reflecting their own perceptions, but also perhaps linked to the age and experience of the performers who they are coaching. Given what we know about growth and development and LTAD, you would expect a coach (in the same sport) to give a different 'ranking' for a 13-year-old female performer, compared to a more experienced adult male performer.

Try Activity 3.

Activity 3

1 Rate the importance of each Performance Factor for your performer/team (be clear about the age and stage of development) from 1 (unimportant) to 5 (very important):

	Unimportant				Very important
Physical	1	2	3	4	5
Technical	1	2	3	4	5
Tactical	1	2	3	4	5
Mental	1	2	3	4	5

2 Now, prioritise these factors, placing the most important against number one and the least important against number four.

1

2

3

4

3 List the factors in the order of importance in your sport for a:

junior (under-18) performer/team

1

2

3

4

international adult performer/team

1

2

3

4

4 Briefly explain why the two lists are the same or why they differ:

There are no correct answers – you may have highlighted the importance of one single factor or you may perceive two or three as being of equal importance. Your perception of the relative importance of these factors will influence the way you plan your coaching programme for a particular performer or team. Every performer is, after all, an individual and has differing levels of ability and skills.

© Alan Edwards

Activity 4

So far, we have considered the Performance Factors, but you already know that there are several different components of each factor (for example, strength or flexibility under Physical or confidence or mistake management in Mental).

Imagine your performer or team producing a perfect performance or reflect on a previous top performance in your sport. List the specific components of each Performance Factor that make up these top performances. Try to think of as many as you can.

Physical	Technical	Tactical	Mental

Now turn over.

You have probably listed a range of components for each Performance Factor. This demonstrates the variety of components that contribute to top performance – there are no right or wrong answers. This information will help you to develop your annual plan and will be used in many of the activities as you work through this resource. You have probably identified some of the following components:

Physical Components

- *endurance*
- *speed*
- *power*
- *flexibility*
- *strength*

Technical Components *(will depend on sport)*

- *match-winning shots (netball)*
- *backstroke – arm action (swimming)*
- *return of serve (badminton)*
- *length of stride (running)*
- *passing skills (football)*
- *scrummage skills (rugby)*

Tactical Components *(will depend on sport)*

- *patterns of play (volleyball)*
- *race and pace (swimming)*
- *assessment of opposition strengths and weaknesses (netball)*
- *use of game/match plan (cricket)*

Mental Components

- *motivation*
- *relaxation*
- *anxiety control*
- *concentration*
- *confidence*
- *commitment.*

Remember, in designing a training programme, you will need to include the right quantity of all of the different components in each Performance Factor – too much of one, too little of another or leaving one out could lead to the performer being overtrained or undertrained. Remember, too, that the relative importance of these components will vary according to the time of year, the sequencing of activities, the level at which the performer/team competes, the age of the performer and the goals the performer/team have set for the season or year. If you are working with junior performers, then some components may simply not be possible for them because of their stage of development. Knowledge of growth and development and LTAD is therefore essential if you are developing programmes for junior performers. There are several sports coach UK resources listed at the end of this section that refer specifically to these issues.

If you are involved in a multi-sport (eg triathlon), you will have to consider the requirements of each event. If you are coaching a team game, you will need to examine each position, identify its specific demands and then plan your programmes accordingly. The individual requirements of a front-row forward in rugby are, for example, very different from those of a scrum-half or fullback. The demands on the goalkeeper in hockey are different from those on the forwards.

If your sport has a strong tactical emphasis, you will need to highlight particular tactical components when you coach, in line with your game plan. However, it will be important to plan training sessions very carefully so that every component is included to achieve 'multiple' outcomes. A football coach, for example, although selecting particular components and physical attributes as important, depending on his vision of the ideal game plan for the team, will also ensure that others are included in a training session. Different football coaches could have very different perspectives on the important technical and tactical, or even physical and mental, components, depending on whether the game plan they use is based on possession or pressure. This is also true of other tactical sports.

2.2 Analysing the Components of the Performance Factors

In the last activity, you were asked to break down the Performance Factors into their different components. In order to assess and develop performance in many of these components, it will often be necessary to break the components down even further, as shown in the examples below.

A gymnastics coach probably needs to identify different sub-components of flexibility, in order to assess performers more accurately, to then plan a more detailed programme.

Performance Factor: Physical skills

Component: Flexibility in gymnastics

Sub-components:

Hip abduction	Hip flexion	Hip extension
Shoulder abduction	Shoulder flexion	Shoulder extension
Spine abduction	Spine flexion	Spine extension

A tennis or badminton coach will want to break down the technical skill of serving, in order to increase racket-head speed to get more power.

Performance Factor: Technical skills

Component: Serve in badminton or tennis

Sub-components:

Racket-head speed – Use of the kinetic chain (generating force from the ground to the large muscle groups of the legs and trunk and finally to the smaller muscles of the shoulder, elbow and wrist)

Grip

External and internal rotation of the shoulder

Ball placement

Activity 5

In Activity 4, you listed a range of components which made up a top performance in your sport. This activity asks you to analyse each of these components to determine the key sub-components in your sport. Examples from different sports are included to guide you.

Performance Factors

Technical

Components	Sub-components
eg netball – individual ball skills	passing, shooting, handling
eg cricket – batting skills	back lift, swing path, follow-through

Physical

Components	Sub-components
eg basketball – speed	reaction speed, acceleration speed, agility
eg swimming – flexibility (backstroke)	dorsi/plantarflexion (ankles), hyperextension/flexion (lower back), posterior/anterior shoulder mobility

Tactical

Components	Sub-components
eg rugby union – for outside half	awareness of game plan, variety, adaptability, options, timing
eg football – keeping possession	positioning, timing movement, spatial awareness

Mental

Components	Sub-components
eg squash – decision making	speed of thought, calmness, awareness, selection of options, prioritisation
eg archery – self-confidence	self-belief, positive thoughts, high commitment, strong focus

Now turn over.

25

This activity required you to draw on your knowledge of different components - sport physiology, psychology and biomechanics - as well as the technical and tactical factors of your sport. It may have helped you to identify some areas in which you need to improve or refresh your knowledge. Perhaps you are unsure of the latest tactical or technical variations in your sport? 2.5 Recap and What Next? directs you to sources of further information.

2.3 Assessing Your Performer/Team

Once you have identified the relative importance of the Performance Factors and their components in your sport, you are in a position to determine the level of ability of your performers in each of them. This will then give you a starting point for your planning process.

You now need to assess where performers are in order to plan for where they want to be. You must decide where and how you can gather information about each Performance Factor and its components. This could be during training, in a laboratory setting or during a competition. All three environments have advantages and limitations, in terms of assessment and gathering information. The important issue is to make sure that the information you get from your assessment is as realistic to the performer and the sport as possible.

Assessing in different environments

Assessment can be difficult, for example, during competition, because all the Performance Factors blend together into a whole and this may mask small deficiencies. Is it possible to assess whether a footballer's flexibility is sufficient to minimise the potential for injury, just by watching match play? Is it possible to assess aerobic endurance accurately during a long-distance canoe race? So coaches will need to combine different assessment methods in different environments, to gather the information they require. You will need to be sure that the methods you use for young performers are indeed a real measure of their skill, fitness and potential in any given factor. There is an element of 'wait and it will happen' with young performers who are developing rapidly, especially through puberty. So, while an assessment will give you an indication, it may not be necessary or wise to train that component just yet.

Whatever method of assessment is used, it is important to bear the objective in mind – to give information about where the performer/team is *now* and plan for progress towards the goal.

Laboratory versus field testing

Many coaches believe that laboratory tests are of more benefit than field-based tests, because they are more accurate, control more variables, and so should be more reliable. These factors must be weighed against others, such as the difficulty of reproducing the demands of the sport situation in the laboratory (lack of specificity), the possible influence of an alien environment on motivation or the expense and logistical difficulties of using a laboratory. There are arguments for and against both types of test. The test you select should be the one which best suits your needs and, in some cases, this will be the one that most resembles the competitive situation.

Direct/indirect assessment

Some components can be assessed directly. Aerobic endurance, for example, can be assessed directly, through measurement of the subject's VO_2max[1] in the laboratory or fitness centre. It may also be assessed indirectly by the Multistage Fitness Test[2] in the training environment.

Concentration, though, can probably only be measured *indirectly*, through error counts in the training or competition environment or by subjective assessment in questionnaires.

Objective/subjective assessment

Your assessment can be objective or subjective, depending on how you gather the information you want. *Objective assessments* are based on empirical evidence, such as times or scores. *Subjective assessments* depend on your impression of the performance (eg you believe that the hockey goalkeeper's clearances were an effective means of building an attack, but you have no figures to prove it). Most coaches need empirical information to support their thoughts about performance and so they will use some form of objective assessment. Performance assessments can take many forms, some of which are included in the table overleaf.

© www.actionplus.co.uk

[1] A test to measure the volume of oxygen a performer consumes per minute of maximal activity – it is a valid test of aerobic endurance capacity.

[2] A progressive shuttle running test to exhaustion – see 2.5 Recap and What Next? for details of the Multistage Fitness Test.

Table 1: Methods of performance measurement

Method	Application	Example
Notational/ video analysis	This can be used to measure the efficacy of techniques/tactical decisions/mental skills.	• Accuracy of distribution by footballer • Line-out success rates in rugby union • Use of routines in tennis
Biomechanical analysis	This can be used to measure all aspects of the technical efficiency of a performer.	• Throwing technique for a javelin competitor • Sprint technique analysis for a runner
Psychological testing	Mental skills and attitudes are difficult to assess directly and objectively, though indirect and subjective measures are available.	• Standardised interviews • Validated questionnaires (SCAT – Sport Competition Anxiety Test) • Behavioural observations (eg comparison of success rates in training and competition)
Sport-specific skills testing	Many sports have developed tests for specific skills – refer to your own governing body.	• Passing accuracy in hockey • First ball accuracy in volleyball • Free throws in basketball
Laboratory or fitness-centre-based testing	Tests in a lab or fitness centre can assess almost any component.	• VO_2max measures aerobic endurance • Wingate test measures anaerobic endurance
Field-based fitness testing	Most fitness components can be assessed directly or indirectly in the specific sport environment.	• The Multistage Fitness (bleep) Test (an indirect measure of aerobic endurance – not necessarily a test for young performers) • Blood lactate testing • The vertical jump (an indirect measure of power output – since it is a measure of power, coaches should remember that young performers moving through puberty do not have much muscle strength during the growth spurt and so may have a lower vertical jump simply for reasons of immaturity, rather than ability – this could change quite quickly as they mature)

© www.actionplus.co.uk

2.4 Planning an Assessment Programme

The assessment of a performer's abilities and skills should be well planned. Obviously, before implementing a programme of assessment, the coach must establish some key issues:

1 The Performance Factors to assess (based on a sound knowledge of the sport and the performer)
2 The specific components or sub-components to assess (bearing in mind the age and stage of the performer)
3 The appropriate assessment for each component
4 How to analyse and interpret the results of the assessment.

Assessing the performance factors

We have already established that sports place different emphases on different Performance Factors, so it could make sense to have a programme of assessment based on the principal needs of your sport. The difficulty with this approach is that the Performance Factors are interlinked. For example, technical development often needs physical skill levels to be high; the execution of tactical abilities may depend on appropriate mental skills. A second factor to consider is the age of performers. Juniors may, for example, simply not have the necessary physical abilities to perform some technical skills or the necessary mental skills to use sound (adult) tactics.

Assessing the components or sub-components

You will want as much relevant and accurate information as possible, so it would make sense to assess as many components as possible. However, common sense dictates that testing should not take up too much training time. There needs to be a distinction made between which components are necessary and which would be nice to assess. Plan your programme of assessment around this decision. Some components may be assessed easily and inexpensively. Others are difficult to assess accurately, may be expensive or information could be gathered indirectly. Bear in mind, too, the age and stage of the performer and decide whether, at this time in the development process, an assessment is necessary.

Appropriate assessment methods

Assessments can provide good-quality, useful information, but must be selected systematically and fit the component. In other words, you need to know that the assessment is assessing what you need to know, that the results are dependable and will help you to plan for the future, so it is essential that the assessment process is **valid, reliable and objective**.

Validity is a complex concept. It means the specific inferences taken from the test results are appropriate, meaningful and useful. For an assessment to be valid, the assumption is made that the results allow you to draw accurate conclusions about the performance (eg physical, mental, technical) status of your performer. For example, a test of absolute strength, such as a one-rep maximum (1RM – the amount of weight that can be lifted once only) on a bench press, might be an inappropriate assessment for a gymnast. If it were calculated in terms of a strength/weight ratio, then the result would be more meaningful.

The **reliability** of an assessment refers to the consistency of results over a number of tests:

• on the same occasion (repeatability)

• on different occasions (reproducibility).

Imagine the disparity of results if a 12-minute run were performed on dry, firm grass in summertime and on a wet, muddy surface in winter.

Objectivity is a measure of the degree of agreement between two or more different assessors on a particular assessment. Objectivity is desirable so that different assessors conduct the same test and produce similar, or preferably identical, results. For example, it can be difficult for two people to administer skinfold calipers in an identical manner. Objectivity is very important in fitness testing and can be increased by using:

• accurate electronic timing or measuring devices which eliminate human error

• clearly defined and strictly enforced protocols (eg when using the Multistage Fitness Test, it is important to stop performers if they miss the bleep on two consecutive turns).

Finding the right test

Using a test which has been developed for the specific component you wish to assess is usually better than inventing your own[1]. Tests that have been professionally developed have addressed the issues of validity and reliability. Your governing body of sport should assist you in searching for appropriate tests. Alternatively, BASES[2] (the British Association of Sport and Exercise Sciences) will direct you to an individual qualified in the appropriate field. (See footnote for contact details for BASES, and the Recap and What Next? subsection at the end of this section for a list of publications that include references to tests and testing procedures.)

[1] For further information on designing a fitness testing programme, you are referred to the sports coach UK 'Field-based Fitness Testing' workshop and the resource *A Guide to Field-based Fitness Testing*, complimentary with the workshop or available from Coachwise 1st4sport (tel 0113-201 5555 or visit www.1st4sport.com).

[2] For a list of accredited sport and exercise scientists you should contact The British Association of Sport and Exercise Sciences (BASES), Leeds Metropolitan University, Carnegie Faculty of Sport and Education, Fairfax Hall, Headingley Campus, Beckett Park, Leeds LS6 3QS. Tel: 0113-283 6162. Website: www.bases.org.uk

Activity 6

Enter the preferred method of assessment for all the components and sub-components of the Performance Factors that you identified in Activity 5. If you do not intend to assess a component, draw a line through the box. Examples are given for some assessments:

Component	Assessment Method	Assessment Venue		
		Laboratory	Field	Competition
Endurance	Multistage Fitness Test		✓	
Speed	30-metre sprint		✓	
Concentration	TAIS (Nideffer, 1976)	✓		

Using different tests

Sports coaches sometimes have a narrow perspective of testing, and can focus solely on fitness testing or technical assessments. However, there are a number of tests available for almost every component in a Performance Factor. For example, most coaches know how and when to use fitness tests and some are aware of the potential of mental-skills assessments and biomechanical assessments. Other areas, such as medical screening and nutritional assessments, are neglected in some sports, especially for junior performers. However, these can highlight any factors (personal or lifestyle) which may predispose the performer to an increased risk of injury and illness, either during training or competition.

Medical screening can help to quantify the stresses your performer is likely to face during training or competition, or whether your performer's anatomical structure is able to cope with the imposed stresses of competition/training. It can identify whether or not the performer has any medical issues that will impact on future performance, or even make it unsafe for that performer to take part in exercise or sport. A number of sports ensure that their young performers undertake stringent heart tests in order to identify any problems.

A dietary assessment can provide a detailed insight into nutritional practices and help assess:

• the adequacy of the performer's diet, in terms of overall energy consumption, specific nutrient requirements or additional vitamins and minerals that may be needed, together with the adequacy of hydration

• how to plan menus around lifestyle (eg shift/night workers, early-morning training)

• whether any specific dietary manipulation is required (eg to counteract weight loss or gain).

The essential requirements of an effective nutritional assessment and subsequent nutrition plan are that they are sport-specific and tailored to your performer's needs.

Notational and video analysis

Competitions can be used to gather information on the current state of preparation of a performer or team. In many sports (such as field games), a coach may need to use the competitive situation to gather information that cannot be gathered in training, because of the difficulty in simulating opposition. However, because of the complexity of many games, an objective measurement of some components of performance is often very difficult to obtain. How can a team's defensive performance be analysed objectively, for example? You could seek indicators based on individual elements of performance, such as tackles made or possession turnovers, which can be measured and documented. Video analysis and notational analysis techniques allow you to focus on a specific aspect of performance and gather information on it.

The information generated through video or notational analysis is vital to the assessment of individual players and teams and will provide much information that you will require to plan or adjust training programmes. It can be used to identify strengths and weaknesses and measure them objectively. This enables you to make judgements which are based on facts and figures, rather than relying on subjective assessments of the situation. In team games, notational and video analysis have become key mechanisms for the analysis of the performance of players and opponents.

Video analysis is used for the assessment of many different components of performance – technical, tactical and mental/behavioural. Depending on the video analysis system used, you can then, for example, assess different components in slow motion or group specific plays in a game together (eg first serves in tennis, specific gates on a slalom course in skiing, moves/positioning by players in basketball).

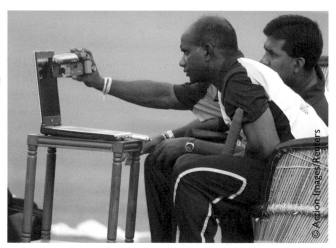

© Action Images/Reuters

Notational analysis can be a laborious process, but can be greatly helped by the use of computer software programs. There are a number of different programs available to the coach. The use of paper notational analysis sheets is, for reasons of cost, the most accessible form of match or game analysis. These may be filled out while the game or match is in progress. Usually, this task can be delegated to trusted assistants or even parents of young performers. Whatever the method used, it is essential to decide beforehand what to record. Simplicity is usually the best answer. Information can be recorded numerically (number of passes, plays, scores, first serves, etc), diagrammatically (line drawings of moves, patterns of play, etc) or by listing specific events. Notational analysis can focus on team performance or on individuals. Most coaches choose to draft their own notational analysis sheets, so the information they acquire is specific to their own needs.

When compiling a notational analysis sheet:

• identify the component of performance you want to analyse/measure

• decide on the specific criteria you will use to measure that component

• determine the exact parameters you will use to define these criteria

• decide how these criteria will be recorded

• ensure that the recording process is as simple as possible and manageable in real time.

Here is an example of a notational analysis sheet that a rugby coach might decide to use, in accordance with the above procedure:

Notes

• I want to analyse turnovers of our possession to attempt to identify patterns.

• A turnover occurs if possession changes hands without a score occurring.

• Turnovers may occur in open play, if we take the ball out of play or if a scrum is awarded to the opposition from our possession.

• This process will be recorded by my assistant coach during the game.

Set Play	Position on Pitch	First-phase Play	No. of Phases	Player Losing Possession	Reason for Loss
Kick-off	B3	Kick to box	1	9	Kick too long
Line-out	C3	Kick to touch	1	10	Safety play
Line-out	B3	Strike channel 1(12)	4	2	Poor body position in tackle

Such information could provide the coach with objective feedback on the patterns and reasons for his team losing possession. It would allow him to give feedback to his players and to pinpoint specific problems. Examples of other match analysis sheets for rugby union are provided on page 34.

An example of a 'flow chart' analysis sheet which can be used in tennis is also given. This chart shows the sequence (flow) of points won and lost in a number of games in the match. It can be used by the coach to assess a variety of different components, for example, the ability of the player to sustain momentum in a match, to record points won on serve or return or when mental confidence was shown. A different form of notational analysis, such as a numerical chart, would be used to record the number of first serves or patterns of service return and this is shown on page 36.

Scrums to Leicester

Zone	Back/Wheel Forward/Stable/Penalty/Free Kick	Push Over	Move Left	Move Right	Backs				Kicks				Ball Carrier	Success/Fail
					CH1	CH2	CH3	Blind Side	Tough	High	Position	Drop	Behind Defence	

Line-outs to Leicester

Zone	No. of Men	Throw to	F. Kick Won/Lost/Void/Penalty	Maul/CT/Def/Ruck/Loose	Used by Forwards	Kick				Backs			Success/Fail
						Tough	High	Position	Drop	C1	C2	C3	

Figure 3: Match analysis sheets for rugby union

Name of player Mary Kate Brown		Opponent Joanne Smith		Venue		Event girls' 14s
1-0	1-1	2-1	3-1	3-2	4-2	5-2
serve	receive	serve	receive	serve	receive	serve
						W
						W W
						o o
				W		W W W
			x W	W o		o o o
			x W	W o o	x	W o o
			x L	W o o	x	W o
	W	W	L	W o	W	
	W	W		L	L	
W W	L					
L	L					
W W	W o W					
	L o L					

Figure 4: Match flow chart for tennis

W = point won   o = double fault – concentration?

L = point lost   x = 2nd serve return down line

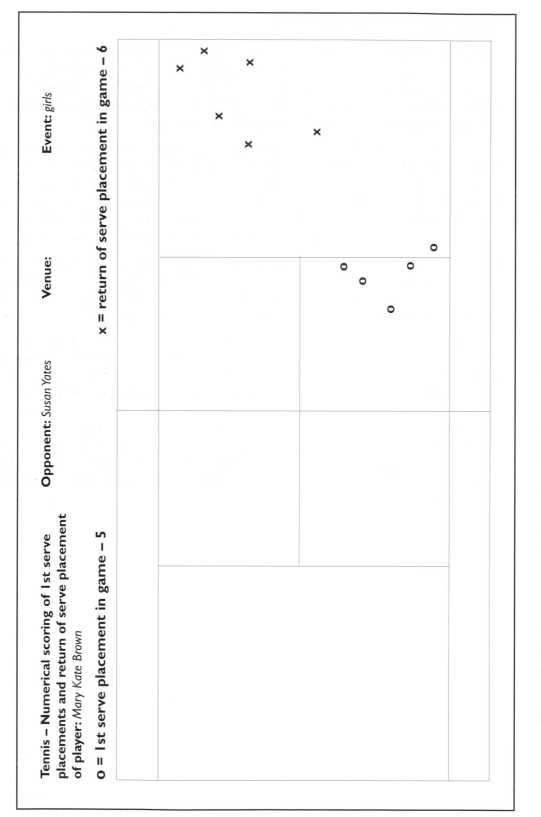

Tennis – Numerical scoring of 1st serve
placements and return of serve placement
of player: *Mary Kate Brown*

Opponent: *Susan Yates*   Venue: Event: *girls*

o = 1st serve placement in game – 5

x = return of serve placement in game – 6

Figure 4: Tennis – numerical scoring of first-serve placements and return-of-serve placements

The key issue for you, therefore, in choosing the correct means of assessment is to decide the best, most reliable, valid and simplest means of assessing your performer or team, in order to plan training around the components of the Performance Factors.

Analysing and interpreting the assessment results

Gathering the information is sometimes the easy part of evaluating performance. The information must then be interpreted and a judgement made on the performer or team. Although the process of analysing and interpreting the results of valid, reliable and objective assessments may appear fairly straightforward, *subjective* judgements often need to be made on the basis of the information collected.

There are a multitude of factors that affect performance in tests, only some of which can be controlled by the tester. Factors such as unfamiliarity, perception of others (especially with junior performers), motivation and anxiety can cause the results to vary considerably. It is important to remember that the results of tests are also very much secondary to performance in competition. An undue emphasis on performance in tests can be anxiety-inducing in the performer and coach and skew the perceptions of both.

Therefore, one of the most important aspects of assessments is the *perception of the result by the performer*. It is vital to give positive feedback to your performers about any tests carried out. The way in which the information gathered is analysed and fed back to the performer will determine whether it has a positive or negative effect on motivation.

It is also essential when working with young performers who are not yet through puberty to understand the importance of chronological and developmental (biological) age. It is very easy for comparisons to be made with other performers of the same chronological age, or even with the performances of adult performers. With young performers, such comparisons are meaningless, but results of tests (especially fitness tests) have an impact on the individual performer. The issues of possible two-year developmental variation above or below the chronological age, as well as different rates of growth, are very important, particularly during adolescence. Therefore, it is important to emphasise that the only comparisons that should be made are with the outcomes of the individual's previous assessment.

© Alan Edwards

Activity 7

Jot down any factors that might affect a performer's perceptions of test results.

Now turn over.

You may have thought of:
- *the coach's opinion or perception of the scores*
- *the age of the performer*
- *other performers' opinions or perceptions of the scores*
- *the score in relation to the performer's specific goals and more general aspirations*
- *the gender of the performer.*

Performers' rationalisation of test results can also provide an insight into the state of their self-confidence. Both positive and negative results can be attributed to internal ('I felt good today/felt poorly today') or external factors ('I ate the wrong food this morning/I never do well at this track!'). In general, elite performers (because they tend to have high levels of self-confidence) attribute blame for poor results to external factors, and assume the credit for good results themselves. This is a mechanism to protect their self-confidence. If their reasoning is contrary to this, it may be worth investigating.

The coach will interpret the scores in relation either to previous assessments or to norms that the governing body of sport may have and other performers will tend to compare results with their own. For your performer(s), the interpretation of the results will depend on a combination of their own expectations and their perceptions of other people's reactions.

The vital impact that assessments have on the planning of training programmes should now be very apparent. You can use the information gathered as baseline information to plan your performers' programmes of preparation. *You know where the performers are. Your programme should be designed to take them towards their goals.* You will need to use many of the same assessments on a regular basis, to set goals and monitor your performers' progress towards their goals. This will be discussed in Section 7.

2.5 Recap and What Next?

This section has encouraged you to:

- think carefully about the specific demands of your sport – this is a very necessary process for all coaches, so that training programmes are as complete as possible, 'fit' the sport and leave nothing to chance
- assess your performers on an individual basis in the context of these demands – performer assessment is the first step in the planning of coaching programmes
- consider how the performers perceive their needs.

The following packs may be useful in building your knowledge of the information in Section 2 and are available from Coachwise 1st4sport (0113-201 5555 or www.1st4sport.com):

Brewer, C. (2005) *Strength and Conditioning for Games Players*. Leeds: Coachwise Business Solutions/The National Coaching Foundation. ISBN: 978-1902523-85-9.

Farrally, M. (2003) *An Introduction to the Structure of the Body*. 2nd edition. Leeds: Coachwise Business Solutions/The National Coaching Foundation. ISBN: 978-1850601-69-2.

Farrally, M. (2005) *An Introduction to Sports Physiology*. 2nd edition. Leeds, Coachwise Business Solutions/The National Coaching Foundation. ISBN: 978-947850-98-6.

Higham, A. (2000) *Momentum: The Hidden Force in Tennis*. Oxford: Meyer and Meyer Sport. ISBN: 978-1841260-40-2.

The National Coaching Foundation (2005) *Multistage Fitness Test*. Leeds: Coachwise Business Solutions/The National Coaching Foundation.

Sellars, C. (2004) *Mental Skills: An Introduction for Sports Coaches*. Leeds: Coachwise Business Solutions/The National Coaching Foundation. ISBN: 978-947850-34-1.

sports coach UK (2002) *Physiology and Performance*. 3rd edition. Leeds: Coachwise Business Solutions/The National Coaching Foundation. ISBN 978-947850-24-4.

Stafford, I. and Balyi, I. (2005) *Coaching for Long-term Athlete Development*. Leeds: Coachwise Business Solutions/The National Coaching Foundation. ISBN: 978-1-902523-70-9.

Further reading

Nideffer, R.M. (1976a) 'Test of attentional and interpersonal style', *Journal of Personality and Social Psychology*, 34: 394–404.

Nideffer, R.M. (1976b) *The Inner Athlete*. New York: Thomas Crowell. ISBN: 978-0-690009-61-3

Section 3 gives you information from the performer's viewpoint and will develop the concepts of profiling and goal setting, to ensure that the programme of preparation you plan is consistent with your performers' or team's perceptions of their needs.

Section 3

Information About the Performer/Team

3.0 What this Section is About

In the previous section, we looked at the Performance Factors in relation to planning programmes for performers and teams in your sport. High-level performance in any sport depends on reaching high standards in the Performance Factors and their components. As a coach, you will need to know the relative importance of the different factors at different stages of performer development and know how to assess them in a sport-specific way. Without this information, programme planning at any level is meaningless, but sport is essentially about the performers who take part. Coaches can develop good programmes, but without the performers to use them, they cannot come to life. So you also need specific information about the performers themselves – who and where they are developmentally and what their goals and ambitions are. This section will help you to obtain:

1 information about your performers or team

2 information from goal setting – what your performers or team want to achieve in a given period of time.

It might seem obvious, but for any plan or programme to be effective, it *must* be *relevant, realistic and acceptable* to the performers.

Coaches frequently encounter challenges with performers who seem to have less than perfect motivation, don't listen and have a poor attitude to training. One reason for all of these challenges is that the coach and performer have different perceptions of the performer's priorities and abilities. It should be remembered that performers take part in sport for different reasons. For many, especially young performers, the sport 'just happened'. They began in school or in a local club, enjoyed it, improved and began to develop ambitions. Others may have taken up a sport because their friends or their parents wanted them to do so. It is vital as a coach to know *why* your performers are taking part and to realise that, for many, elite performance is not an ambition. They may simply want to enjoy their sport and so will need high-quality sessions and short-term programmes, rather than quadrennial or annual plans. In order to better understand your performers, there are two methods that can help you as a coach. The first is *performance profiling* and the second is *goal setting*. Some coaches use performance profiling to help them understand how their performers perceive themselves and their performances and learn why they take part in the sport. Profiling helps ensure that both you and your performers are working to the same agenda.

Goal setting of long-, medium- and short-term goals enables a plan to be broken down into manageable steps. When goal setting is also based on a performance profile, you can be certain that the goals you set with your performers are relevant to them and that their programme is realistic and acceptable

By the end of this section, you should be able to:

• explain performance profiling

• use performance profiling to generate a profile of your performers/team

• understand the role of goal setting to focus your programmes on performer needs.

3.1 Performance Profiling

Performance profiling[1] sets a profile of your performer/team against the Performance Factors in your sport. It is a tool that helps you as a coach to understand your performers' perceptions of their strengths and weaknesses in the Performance Factors. This information can then be used to identify any differences in perception between you and your performers about their performance.

Performance profiling is, therefore, a useful exercise for ensuring that performer and coach are working to the same agenda. It can also be used to prioritise different components for an individual performer when planning the training programme. Some coaches will also use profiling as a mechanism for monitoring progress towards a performer's or team's goals.

Performance profiling in team sports

Coaches in team sports will need to complete the profiling exercise at two levels. They will profile their team to generate a collective perspective on strengths and weaknesses. This can be a powerful tool for ensuring that the team members are on the same wavelength and share the same philosophy. The exercise can also identify the team's perceptions of their ability to use different game plans and tactics, which can often be different from that of the coach.

Team coaches might also profile each individual within their squads. All players will have perceptions about their strengths and weaknesses, which may or may not be in line with those of the coach. Disagreements on selection policy and training-programme content can be minimised if coaches understand players' perception of their performances.

[1] Further details can be found in *Performance Profiling*, available from Coachwise 1st4sport (tel 0113-201 5555 or visit www.1st4sport.com).

Creating the individual profile

There are some important procedural steps to follow when completing a performance profile. The process must be led by the performer and requires the following:

1   The identification and listing of the qualities which describe high-level performance.

    *It is important that these qualities are generated by the performer without any direction. Some assistance may be needed initially, but the coach should **not** lead the discussion.*

2   Clarification of exactly what the performer means by each quality.

    It is easy to misconstrue a performer's meaning, or to impose your own interpretation on a term the performer is using in a different context, so clarification is essential.

3   A statement of a personal rating on these qualities, from 1–10.

    Again, the rating should be made by the performer without any assistance from the coach. Ten should represent the highest level that the performer believes is achievable.

4   Plotting of the scores on the profile chart.

5   The same scale being used to plot the goal to be achieved in 12 months' time.

    This should be used as an indication of the performer's priorities.

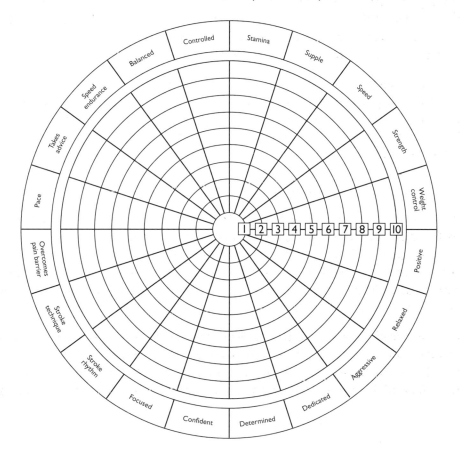

Figure 6: Profile chart generated by a swimmer

Activity 8

1 Ask your performer to select the 20 most important qualities required to achieve a top performance in your sport. Write them in the space below. There is no need to rank them.

1		11	
2		12	
3		13	
4		14	
5		15	
6		16	
7		17	
8		18	
9		19	
10		20	

2 Transfer the 20 qualities listed in part one of the exercise to the perimeter of the following blank profile (if repeating the exercise with different performers, use a separate profile for each one). Use the example of the swimmer as a guide. (Refer to Appendix C where a full-page version is available.)

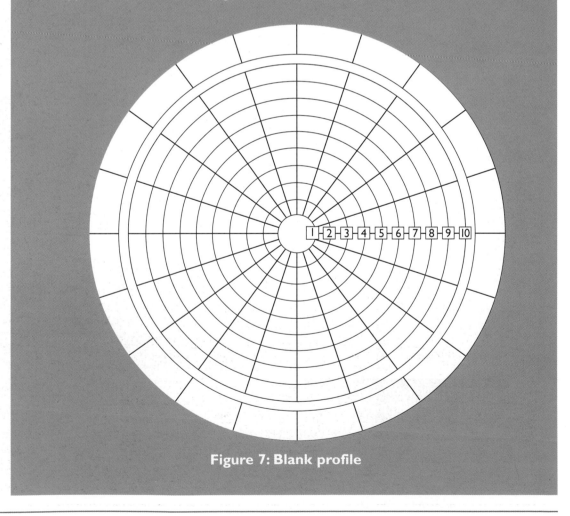

Figure 7: Blank profile

Activity 9

Now, your performer should use a rating scale (1–10) for each quality, as shown on the netball goalkeeper's profile below.

Not at all   Very much

| 1 | 2 | 3 | 4 | 5 | 6 | 7 | 8 | 9 | 10 |

Two guidelines help in developing the rating scale:

• Do not spend too long analysing each quality – trust the first impression or feeling.

• Try to use the whole range of the scale.

Get the performer to score each quality and mark the scores on the profile you began to complete in Activity 8 on the previous page. Figure 8 provides an example of this.

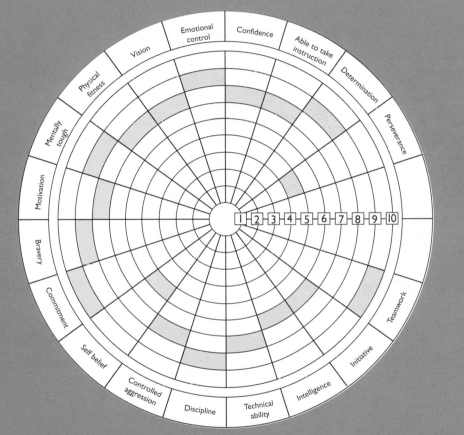

Figure 8: Profile of a netball goalkeeper

The completed profile will now highlight what the performer believes to be the strongest qualities of performance.

In Figure 8, the netball goalkeeper considers herself to be strong on the qualities of **commitment** *and* **teamwork***, so the training programme, and especially the way in which the coach interacts with the player in individual sessions, should build on these two strengths. The* **profile** *also highlights the weak areas as* **self-belief** *and* **perseverance***. This information would help you as a coach to structure the training programme to help this player improve in these areas.*

3.2 Team Profiling

The reasons for completing a team profile are very similar to those for the individual profile. The problem lies in the identification of a common consensus from a large number of individuals on their self-perceptions. This process is an important step in team building, so teams that are in a later stage of development – that have played together for some time and have very clear ambitions for the future – should find the process easier. The activity could also accelerate the team-building process in a new team, by developing a shared understanding of the important qualities for team performance and by enhancing performers' awareness of themselves as a group of people with a common set of goals. The following steps are a suggestion for introducing the activity, but you may wish to adjust them to suit your team and circumstances:

1 Generate a list of the qualities the team believes to be important for team success. Bear in mind the characteristics of a top team in your sport, as well as your own team when it is successful. This is best completed in an open brainstorming session where all contributions are valid and noted.

2 Clarify what is meant by each quality.

3 Individuals rank the top five qualities they believe to be the most important for their team's success (one being the most important).

4 Assign points to each quality, according to how they have been ranked (from first rank, which is worth five points, down to the fifth rank, which is worth one point).

5 Write the 10 qualities with the most points in the profile chart below.

6 Individuals rate the team from 0–10 for each quality.

7 Mark the average score on the profile chart as the team rating for that quality.

This exercise is an easy one to perform (but may take a little time) and can remove the guesswork from the coach's task of assessing the mood and confidence of the team. It is important that the profiling is completed honestly. You must make it clear that each individual can make an honest and open contribution.

Team Performance Profile

Qualities	1	2	3	4	5	6	7	8	9	10

Key issues in profiling

It is important to appreciate that, when you profile performers and teams, you are dealing with differences between their perceptions of the requirements for top performance and their perceptions of their own performances in relation to these requirements. These may or may not concur with your perceptions. Any gap between your perceptions and your performers' perceptions can create problems for a programme of training and competition and needs resolution at the planning stage, as well as during the training itself.

For younger or more inexperienced performers, this may be a more difficult exercise, simply because they have no real understanding of what high-level sport entails. Therefore, the qualities they identify should be treated with caution, but nonetheless do give you a basis from which to plan.

Consider the boxer whose self-ratings for all the different Performance Factors were three to four points higher than his coach's ratings. Why would that disparity occur? How does one deal with that in planning coaching programmes?

There is no correct answer to the questions that the profiling exercise raises. The disparities in perception are the basis for discussion between the performers and the coach. Discussions should lead to an improved understanding and a shared perspective on performances and training for performance. This shared understanding can then form the basis for the joint planning of a comprehensive programme of training and competition.

Using profiling to prioritise training

Some coaches work on a performer's weaknesses when training and, as competition approaches, spend the final preparation period reinforcing strengths. Other coaches spend more time on developing strengths, in order to keep confidence high all the time, even when weaknesses are addressed. Whatever the approach, the goal is for the performer to be in a positive state of mind before and during competition. The reason to train is to compete. The performance-profiling exercise gives you an indication of the specific needs of each performer and team and provides a record of the performer or team's perceived strengths and weaknesses. In developing a programme based on profiling, you should also identify ways in which coaching and training should be undertaken in order to meet the needs of the performer. For example, in Figure 8, the netball goalkeeper identified clear strengths and weaknesses. The coaching methodology used in individual training sessions, as well as in the approach to competition, should use techniques that enhance the strengths and minimise or eliminate the weaknesses identified by the performer.

3.3 Setting Goals

The assessment of your performers in Section 2 and the profiling exercise in this section have generated a lot of information about your performers that enables you to prioritise and plan your programmes of training and competition.

Both you and your performers will want to improve performance in the areas you have prioritised. A realistic way to further this objective is to set clear and meaningful goals. This process should be a joint exercise between coach and performer. In the case of young performers, who do not have a full appreciation of the requirements and/or are not even sure whether they will stay in the sport, goal setting is still a valuable exercise, but the goals should be short term. It is also a sound idea to include parents when young performers are involved. Provided that performers feel ownership of goals, the process of goal setting can increase your performers' commitment to their training, even in single sessions. In sports and other activities, it has been demonstrated that, when a person has set himself achievable goals, his motivation is increased.

The next subsection will remind you of the important issues when setting goals with your performers. Use the exercises that follow to increase your goal-setting skills. When you set goals for real, remember that they must be set jointly by coach and performer.

Principles of goal setting

A goal is the aim or desired outcome for your efforts in an activity. For sportspeople, goals are the framework on which training for competition is constructed. In Section 1, we referred to performers' dreams and the role of the coach in helping performers get from where they are now to the place where their dreams can be realised. Dreams are unlikely to come true without a clear plan in place to fulfil them. Goal setting is about putting clear, manageable steps in place to help performers to achieve their dreams.

To be effective and give a better chance of performer success, goals should conform to the basic principles outlined in the following panel.

© Alan Edwards

All goals should follow the acronym SMARTER.

S pecific		they should be precise – it is difficult to focus on or measure the success of goals that are vague
M easurable		quantifiable goals can be measured and assessed, and show progress is being made
A greed		goals should be agreed by the performer, coach and others, such as parents, if necessary; the goals are also under the performer's control
R ealistic		goals should be challenging, but within the performer's capability
T ime		each goal should have a specified timescale in which to be achieved – goals usually have short-, medium- or long-term time phases.
E xciting		goals that are enjoyable, challenging and interesting to achieve are more likely to be reached by the performer
R ecorded		goals that are written down (and visible) are more likely to be reached[1].

Identifying SMARTER goals is sometimes tough, but performers in every sport need to apply the same principles to their goal setting. For example, *specific* and *measurable* goals are easier to identify when performance can be directly measured (eg long jump, javelin), timed (eg downhill skiing, cycling) or scored (eg archery, shooting, bowling in cricket). However, with practice and thought, appropriate and quantifiable goals can be set for any sport (eg numbers of turnovers or rebounds in basketball, number of successful backhands in a set in badminton, number of first serves in tennis). Sport psychologists have shown that higher levels of performance occur when the goals set are more specific and challenging. It goes without saying that goals must be set and *agreed* both by the coach and performer.

It is important that goals are both *realistic* and *timed*, especially with younger or less confident performers, for whom success and progress are important. With young performers especially, realistic goals mean taking into account growth and development issues as they mature.

Goals that are not *exciting* – or at least interesting – are unlikely to challenge the performer to improve.

Finally, *writing the goals down*, and even placing them where they can be seen frequently, will help performers to stay focused as they train. Committing goals to paper has been shown to increase adherence to the goals. A performer's training diary is a useful place to record goals.

For elite performers, it is usual to build and record goals around either training or competition, or both. Long-term goals are normally set in the context of important

[1] If you require more information on goal setting, you are referred to Chapter 2 of sports coach UK's resource *Mental Skills: An Introduction for Sports Coaches.* Available from Coachwise 1st4sport (tel 0113-201 5555 or visit www.1st4sport.com).

events (major competitions) or stages in a performer's development (in tennis, this could be reaching a certain ranking that then enables the player to enter a higher level of competition). Medium- and short-term goals will have shorter timescales (a season or shorter cycle) and are often linked to improving performance.

For younger performers – and even for those without an annual or longer-term programme – goal setting is an excellent tool for coaches to use to increase motivation and confidence, because improvement against specific objectives is often rapid in young performers. Many coaches do not use profiling with young performers, but every good coach should use some form of goal setting.

The goal-setting process may be as elaborate or as simple as you like. Often, this will depend on the preferences of your performer. It is important that a similar process for goal setting is used at every stage of the programme, so your performer may become familiar with both the idea and the process.

Activity 10

1 First, ask your performer or team to identify a *dream* goal. For example, a bobsleigh team might like to win the national cup or an oarsman might like to win an Olympic gold medal. The dream goal is something that they would ultimately like to achieve in their career in the sport.

2 Using the qualities prioritised in the performer's profile, set three long-term goals (eg over a season or a year) that will contribute towards achieving the dream goal (make sure each goal follows the SMARTER principles).

Now turn over.

Setting individual goals

The following example is of the swimmer profiled in Figure 6.

The swimmer had a dream of winning the national championships at the end of the next two years. In discussion with his coach, the winning times in the nationals for the previous two years were identified and then the goal was set, based on achieving that time in competition beforehand.

In the performance profile, the weaker qualities were the psychological skills areas of focus, relaxation and control. The swimmer set himself a long-term goal for the last meet of the season (nationals) – that he would remain relaxed and focused throughout the lead-up to the event and during the race itself. Coach and performer agreed that this was achievable. They also agreed on a state anxiety scale questionnaire that they would use as a tool to help them monitor progress in this area. In this way, the goal became measurable.

Obviously, at the beginning of the plan and training period, they were not close to achieving this goal. It was necessary to set some medium-term goals that would allow both coach and performer to track progress towards the long-term goal. Swimmer and coach agreed that controlling thought content in the lead-up to the race and the race itself was the most important skill to develop. The coach identified the technical factors that were most important in each section of the race and a race strategy for thought content was developed based on these, as a medium-term goal.

The swimmer also agreed another medium-term goal, of concentrating on a certain aspect of stroke technique for each split. These goals were staggered through the following months so that, for the first month, the swimmer was attempting to maintain concentration on a specific area of technique for 200m; in the following month, he practised switching focus to another factor for the next 200m and so on.

Other medium-term goals were set which worked towards developing a strong and adaptable pre-race strategy. This again focused on controlling thought content by setting a time schedule for mental and physical routines before the race.

Short-term goals were set for the next competition. The swimmer agreed to log thought patterns in the period leading up to the race and during the race. This would serve as a baseline for further short-term goal setting, moving towards the first set of intermediate goals.

Setting team goals

While it is obvious that individuals within a team will set goals for their own training programme, it is also important that team goals are set. This will be an important part of developing team spirit and cohesion, as well as providing a framework for the development of team skills, tactics and match plans. Team goal setting is rather more difficult than for individuals, but is just as important. Goals for the team should be set communally and democratically (if they are to be accepted), though, as coach, you will want to have a significant input. Team meetings at the beginning of the training year are important forums for the setting of such goals and targets.

3.4 Types of Goal

As you probably know, there are several different types of goal and it is important to know the characteristics of each of them, especially in terms of their effect on performance with different performers.

Outcome goals are goals usually tied to competition. They include:

• coming first

• winning a medal

• reaching a final

• being selected for a team.

This type of goal can often be affected by the performance of others and, therefore, is not completely under the control of the performer. However, some performers are highly ego-driven and assess success through comparison with others[1]. It is therefore important, for example, that a hockey coach should be wary if the team sets a target of winning 75% of the games in a season. This goal could become self-defeating for some players, because it may be outside the players' control to achieve it. Performers' self-confidence may be affected if the goals they have committed themselves to become obviously unachievable in mid-season.

Setting outcome goals with young performers can also be problematic. If all young performers were the same in a sport setting, outcome goals would be realistic. However, as we have discussed before, the differences in chronological and developmental (biological) age mean that, often, it is the early maturers (bigger and stronger young people) who win or make finals and get selected. This means that smaller, less mature and potentially more talented performers lose confidence and can even lose interest in the sport.

Process goals have different objectives. They:

• are specific about what needs to be done in order to be successful, in such a way that success can be measured

• base success on self-improvement in a task

• should be set and linked to each of the Performance Factors

• usually refer to a component of performance, such as holding the right grip on the serve in tennis or keeping the skis aligned in skiing (both technical skills)

• are more likely to be under the control of the performer

• cannot be compared with, or be directly influenced by, another performer's performance

• are more appropriate when coaching young performers.

It is generally better if you and your performers set goals related to relevant performance and process, especially with young performers who are still learning so much and for whom long-term performance is the goal. But with older performers, the combination of both process goals and long-term outcome goals can be a very effective motivational tool. Winning a gold medal or a major championship are the dreams for many performers and the reason why many continue to take part in their sport, so do not dismiss them. Treat such goals with caution and try to ensure that, when they are used, there is a real chance that they will be achieved. Process goals, such as achieving a personal best, are also useful for performers to take into competition.

[1] Further details can be found in Goodger, K. (2007) *'Motivational Lessons from a Coaching Great', coaching edge*, 6: 8–10, available from the sports coach UK Membership department (tel 0113-290 7612).

They can remove the thought of the consequences of performing well or badly. A swimmer or hurdler, for example, achieving a personal best in a competition has still achieved a goal.

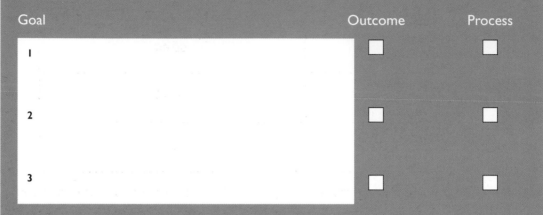

Activity 11

Turn back to Activity 10 (page 53) and assess whether the goals you set were outcome or process goals.

Goal	Outcome	Process
1	☐	☐
2	☐	☐
3	☐	☐

Goals are the structure on which a programme of training and competition should be based. If managed properly, the goal-setting process provides a framework for improving performance through short-, medium- and long-term goals, all of which are developed by the performer. The next activity will require you to construct goals.

Activity 12

Based on your performer profile from Activity 8 (page 46), complete the following:

• Choose a long-term *outcome* goal from Activity 11.

• Set a medium-term goal that will help your performer to achieve this long-term goal.

• Now, set short-term goals that will help your performer to achieve this medium-term goal.

• Set a *process* goal that will be relevant to achieving one of these outcome goals.

Set these goals using the SMARTER principles and bear in mind the commitments of your performers, their situations, needs and other aspirations within the sport.

You will come back to this activity later in the resource.

You should not have found this activity too difficult, as you have identified all the information needed to complete it. It is important that all goals are based on the SMARTER principles.

Goal setting for training sessions

In some sports, like swimming and running, more time is spent training than competing. At an early stage of their development as performers, those under 13 years of age should spend more time training than they do competing, but this ratio changes as the performer gets older. Table 3 on the next page gives the recommended ratios of training to competition at different ages[1].

[1] Further details can be found in Stafford, I. and Balyi, I. (2005) *Coaching for Long-term Athlete Development*: pp. 30–49, available from Coachwise 1st4sport (tel 0113-201 5555 or visit www.1st4sport.com).

Table 2: Recommended ratios of training to competition

Ages	Training to Competition Ratio (%)
Boys: 6–9 years Girls: 6–8 years	No specific ratios, but participation in a wide range of activities is recommended
Boys: 9–12 years Girls: 8–11 years	80:20
Boys: 12–16 years Girls: 11–15 years	60:40
Boys: 16–18 years Girls: 15–17 years	40:60
Boys: 18+ years Girls: 17+ years	25:75

Individual training sessions make up a large part of the time that performers spend in their sport, so goal setting in each and every session is an important motivational tool. As a coach, the more you can involve the performers in the training process, by agreeing short-term goals (that link to other short-term and medium-term goals) for every session, the better. For example, footballers could write a key word, such as *concentration*, on a sticking plaster and then place it on the back of their hand. During the training session, a quick glance at the plaster may encourage them to refocus on their goals. Racket players can count how many times they follow their between-point routine and, paddlers can focus on a specific aspect of their technique during a practice session. Even with younger performers, who might only practise or train in a particular sport for a couple of sessions a week, but play others as well, goal setting is an excellent way to keep them involved in their learning.

As a coach, remember that young performers can learn and improve performance from what they learn and transfer from other sports. This has practical implications for timing when specialised training can and should occur in a particular sport.

3.5 – Recap and What Next?

In each of the Performance Factors, the performance profile and the goal-setting exercises have given you:

- a great deal of information
- the basis of your training plan for your performers/team.

The next section will identify the key training principles so that you can begin the process of developing training plans at different levels.

Further reading

The following resources, which are available from Coachwise 1st4sport (0113-201 5555 or www.1st4sport.com), will complement the information in this section:

Butler, R. (2005) *Performance Profiling.* Leeds: Coachwise Business Solutions/The National Coaching Foundation. ISBN: 978-947850-36-8.

Cabral, P. and Crisfield, P. (2005) *Motivation and Mental Toughness.* 2nd edition. Leeds: Coachwise Business Solutions/The National Coaching Foundation. ISBN: 978-902523-24-5.

Sellars, C. (2004) *Mental Skills: An Introduction for Sports Coaches.* Leeds: Coachwise Business Solutions/The National Coaching Foundation. ISBN: 978-947850-34-1.

Stafford, I. and Balyi, I. (2005) *Coaching for Long-term Athlete Development.* Leeds: Coachwise Business Solutions/The National Coaching Foundation. ISBN: 978-1-902523-70-9.

Section 4

Principles of Training

4.0 What this Section is About

So far in this Part, we have looked at what planning is, and what information you need to plan programmes. So, at this point, we have the information we need to develop every Performance Factor, according to goals set by the performer and you, the coach. There are, however, a number of training principles that ensure that the performer/team reach the goals they have set.

The purpose of training is to progress the performer and bring him or her to a higher level of performance in competition. Training must be incremental and accumulative over time. If the programme is kept at the same level, the performer will *adapt* to that level of training and so will *not* improve or develop. Thus, training is about performers' *adaptation* (for more information see 4.2 The Process of Adaptation in this section) in order to progress towards their goals. It follows that there will be principles that underpin all training. To construct a high-quality programme of training and competition, and the transition between them, the *Principles of Training, and those of adaptation*, must be built into the programme. This section will help you to develop your understanding of these two factors.

By the end of this section, you should be able to:

• outline the principles of training
• explain the physiology and psychology of the adaptation process.

4.1 Principles of Training

As we have noted, the major objective in training is to facilitate the physical and psychological adaptation that improves and optimises performance in competition. Adaptation is dependent upon specific principles being followed. In the training programme, there are several key factors.

© Alan Edwards

Individual differences

Different people will react to training in different ways and at different times. Consider the reactions of young, inexperienced performers approaching training for the first time and a 'seasoned' footballer who has played for many years.

Are you aware of the individual differences between your performers?

Adaptation

The body and mind adapt to the stresses of training by increasing the performer's ability to cope with such stresses. The rate at which different performers adapt is a feature of individual differences.

Are you aware of the adaptation process in each of your performers?

Overload

For adaptation and improvement, the training load must exceed that normally experienced by the performer.

Do you know what training loads are appropriate for different performers and especially young performers at different ages and stages? Is the training load the same for a 12-year-old gymnast as it is for a 21-year-old fast bowler about to represent his country?

Specificity

The adaptation brought on by training will be specific to the type of training undertaken. Specificity is also about training that is specific to the sport. For example, weightlifting is different from weight training, and sprinting is different from marathon running.

What is specific about the training in your sport?

Progression

The training load should be increased progressively to account for the increased capacity of the performer.

Do you know when and how to increase a training load?

Reversibility

Training effects will be lost if they are not maintained by a continuing programme of training. However, the rate at which training effects are lost varies with different components of the Performance Factors.

Do you know which components lose a training effect more quickly or more slowly?

Recovery

Recovery becomes increasingly important as training volumes increase. As young performers mature and move through puberty, you will actually increase the training volume by adding more components of performance to their programme. For adult performers, an increase in the training load will actually mean that the load in each component is increased. Recovery from the training load then becomes a vital aspect of training and preparation.

Do you know how to ensure that young performers who are moving through the growth spurt have enough recovery time?

Variation

Training should be varied, as constant training of the same type will lead to diminishing returns.

Do you know how to vary training programmes to get continuous improvement from individual performers?

In terms of the Principles of Training, perhaps the most important are **specificity**, **progression** and **reversibility**. If you are familiar with the principles which govern adaptation (see 4.2), you will be able to apply these to your performers' training programmes, thus ensuring they get maximum benefit from their training. The next activity will allow you to evaluate your knowledge of the Principles of Training.

Activity 13

Without reference to any other source, try to explain the different Principles of Training with a specific example from your own sport. Try to relate some of your examples to young performers under 18 years of age.

Overload

Example from your sport

Specificity

Example from your sport

Progression

Example from your sport

Reversibility

Example from your sport

Recovery

Example from your sport

Variation

Example from your sport

Now turn over.

Read through the following explanations carefully to see how much you have remembered. You might wish to highlight anything you omitted.

Overload

For a training session to have the desired effect, the demand of the activity must take the performer out of the comfort zone. However, it is important that the training load is appropriate for each person. Too much can cause pain, injury and, ultimately, overtraining or burnout. Too little will mean no gain.

Achieving the appropriate overload requires the skilful manipulation of **training volume** and **intensity**. The volume (amount) of training will be determined by the frequency and duration of the training sessions. The intensity of a training session is a measure of how close to the maximum the performer is performing.

The three variables of **frequency, intensity** and **time (duration)**, will determine the training overload.

Balancing training volume and intensity is very important. Performers are not able to maintain workloads of high intensity for long periods of time, but they should be training at a maximum intensity as competition approaches. In terms of strength or weight training, for example, the volume of training is determined by the number of exercises, sets and repetitions performed per session (duration) and how often the sessions occur (frequency). The intensity of training depends on the percentage of the performer's maximum lift that is being lifted. To achieve the appropriate overload, the coach will manipulate the number of exercises, resistance, number of repetitions or the number of sessions per week (but not all at the same time).

In mental and technical training, an overload on the performer's concentration levels might require the coach to increase the number of potential distractions. For example, a rugby goal kicker might practise goal-kicking skills on a busy training pitch or with a number of distractions created by other players.

Specificity

Adaptation will follow the specific loads or stresses which are placed on the performer. For example, to improve passing skills under pressure, a rugby player must practise under conditions of limited time and space; for a marathon runner to improve aerobic fitness, the aerobic system must be worked; to help football players cope with the stress imposed by a crowd, they need to develop coping skills and be given opportunities to practise in front of crowds. Adaptations in all these areas will be specific to the activity performed in training. For example, a runner who has developed a high maximal oxygen uptake will not necessarily have a similar level when he runs or swims, because different muscle groups are exercised. A basketball playmaker who has developed a high level of confidence in his passing ability will not necessarily approach a different situation – eg shooting for goal – with the same high level of confidence. It follows, therefore, that different performers within the same sport will need specific and individual programmes.

Progression

As the performer's capacity increases through training, even higher demands must be made if improvements are to continue. For example, a tennis player receiving serve may be at a stage of development where deciding how to return the serve after the ball has crossed the net from the server is still difficult, because of a lack of decision-making skills. The coach will gradually increase the number of cues that the receiver should attend to (for example, where the opponent tosses the ball and, ultimately, the position of the shoulders at the start of the service action) until the performer is capable of selecting the right cue and returning more effectively, because a high-quality decision has been made earlier.

Reversibility

Essentially, *if you don't use it, you lose it!* If the training load is reduced or stopped completely, the level of adaptation gained will start to fall. In general, **slow-gain** training methods (where the component is improved slowly) have slow loss when training load is cut. Conversely, **fast-gain** methods (eg crash fitness programmes) have rapid losses of improvement when the training is reduced. This means that all performers should train regularly and they should follow maintenance programmes in those components of performance that are not prioritised for the current training or competition period.

Recovery

The relationship between loading and recovery is very important to understand. Rest is perhaps the most important (but most often forgotten) training principle. Heavy training sessions should be followed by lighter ones or even total rest. The transition between a competition phase and a training phase is a time for recovery. Rest and recovery allows the body to adapt to the stresses being placed on it. It is important to remember that the training effect may be apparent at different times. For example, tactical, technical and mental improvement can often be seen during the training itself, but with physical training, the improvement will be seen later. The performer will be faster, stronger and able to train for longer without fatigue. This is because energy stores are replenished and damaged tissue is repaired or replaced *after* a physical-training session. It is essential that sufficient rest is taken between training units for recuperation and replenishment to take place. The more intense the training or the younger the performer, the longer the recovery required.

Recovery does not mean complete rest or inactivity. A swimmer, for example, may work on aerobic endurance in the morning and could recover by working on basic speed and stroke technique in the evening. In Section 6, you will be shown how to integrate and balance the various performance components to provide optimal improvement. When insufficient time is allowed for recovery, *overtraining* can occur – this will be discussed in more detail later in this section.

Variation

The performer will benefit from variety in a training programme and will progress faster as a result. Repetition of the same training schedule can become boring and the performer will not approach training with the same interest or enthusiasm.

Having read this section, you should now check the accuracy of your responses in Activity 13. Specificity, overload and reversibility are important principles[1] to remember in relation to technical, mental, tactical and physical training. However, all components of training are not often considered in terms of the Principles of Training. Ensure you have grasped these ideas before reading further.

4.2 The Process of Adaptation

Training results in changes to the performer. These changes occur throughout the training period, even though there may not be an obvious and immediate improvement. It takes time to adapt to a training load. Repeated loading and fatigue situations are necessary stimuli for adaptations to occur. Therefore, it is important for you to understand the interplay between loading, recovery, training intensity and training volume.

The Overcompensation Model

During a training session, performers begin to experience fatigue and, if they continued for some time, they would not be able to continue at the same intensity. That is, they might not be able to maintain the required concentration or lift the same weight. They would be unable to repeat the training session just undertaken. Remember, too, that for young performers, the length and intensity of training will be very much lower than it is for adults. During the recovery period following training, the adaptations to that training load occur. This process of adaptation is referred to as **super** or overcompensation (Figure 9).

Loading, recovery and overcompensation are the keys to effective training. Training causes fatigue and a temporary reduction in performance. Improvement occurs during the recovery phase when overcompensation takes place. Following this compensation, the performer is able to train at a higher level (ie maintain concentration for longer, lift heavier weights, produce more accurate serves). It is important to note that:

- there may be a loss or weakened training effect if the time interval between training units is too long – overcompensation will be diminished and the performer may regress to the initial level before the subsequent training load is administered
- if the training stimulus is frequently applied with adequate recovery periods, increases in physiological capacity will occur
- if the loads are applied without sufficient recovery time, a chronic stress situation may occur (overtraining).

So it is essential that you, as a coach, understand these principles and try to maintain a balance between optimal training, competition and recovery programmes for your sport and your performer.

[1] If these principles are new to you, or you would like to refresh your memory, you are referred to the sports coach UK 'Fitness and Training' workshop and the *Physiology and Performance* resource, complimentary with the workshop or available from Coachwise 1st4sport (tel 0113-201 5555 or visit www.1st4sport.com).

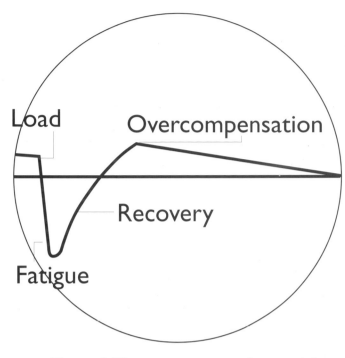

Figure 9: The overcompensation model

The overcompensation model illustrates the effects of training and the resulting fatigue. During the recovery phase, adaptations occur within the system or systems that have been overloaded in the performer and an overcompensation phase (ie increased capacity) can occur. If the performer trains again during this period, then the overcompensation is reinforced and increased. If the performer misses training, there will be a return to the initial level (so the training effect is wasted).

Recovery

We have discussed the importance of recovery and, now, we need to consider how the recovery process can be improved. Recovery should include *physiological* (restoration and regeneration) and *psychological* processes. There are five major ways in which recovery is achieved:

- adherence to work-to-rest ratios
- nutrition and hydration
- sleep
- physical therapies
- the use of psychological techniques.

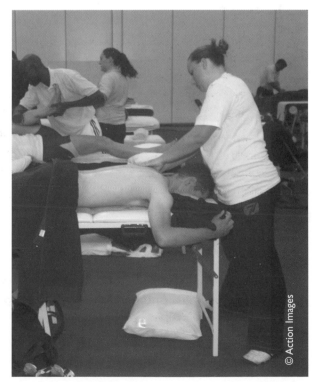

Work-to-rest ratios are important both within and between training sessions. They are the units of work and rest that will best train the performer in that component. For example, a work-to-rest ratio of 1:5 means that, for every unit of work, the performer will take five units of rest. This work-to-rest ratio might apply to speed training with young performers. The ratios depend on the type of work being done. For example, the rest/recovery time between sets/intervals for strength and power development is relatively short and frequent when compared with aerobic training, where they are longer and less frequent. We have already discussed that the body requires recuperation time for adaptation to occur. Consequently, rest periods need to be programmed into training schedules. Sessions should be sequenced (Section 6) to include lighter work within the week, month or cycle, to promote physical adaptation. Rest days, cross training (taking part in other complementary sports) and stretching are all forms of active rest. Psychological regeneration is promoted by giving the mind different types of stimuli. Sleep is important, *both in terms of amount and quality* (see below).

Nutrition and hydration should be given the same consideration as rest and recovery. The body needs enough of the right food (in a well-balanced diet) and fluid at the right time to provide energy for exercise and essential nutrients to help repair exercised muscles. A poor or inadequate diet can lead to fatigue, irritability and perhaps to eating disorders such as anorexia. The body's waste products can indicate whether your performer is eating well and adequately and is well hydrated (eg clear, non-smelling urine is a sign of adequate hydration).

Sleep is a key factor in recovery, restoring the performer both physically and mentally. Sleep deprivation, for personal or other reasons, will affect performance. Performers should be educated in the necessity of maintaining regular hours of sleeping and of maintaining the length of their sleep pattern. When performers travel to a different time zone for competition, time will be needed by the player to adjust physically to the new time zone. Regular sleep patterns should be restored before competition.

A wide range of **physical therapies** can be used to promote restoration (eg hydrotherapies, sports massage). Showers, spa baths, ice baths, hot baths, flotation tanks, saunas and plunge pools are excellent environments in which to stretch and perform self-massage – they increase circulation and provide the sensory stimulation that promotes physiological and psychological recovery. Rehydration is an essential part of recovery, so fluid intake is important during these therapies to prevent dehydration. Sports massage increases blood flow and enhances the delivery of oxygen and nutrients to tired muscles, helping to remove waste products. Massage also helps to warm and stretch soft tissues, providing temporary gains in flexibility. There are also psychological benefits associated with sports massage. As tired and tight muscles relax, there is a corresponding improvement in mood states – the performer feels less fatigued and more relaxed.

Psychological techniques can provide benefits such as increased self-awareness, improved motivation and decreased reactions to stress. A strong relationship exists between physical and mental relaxation – they produce similar responses (lower heart rates and blood pressure, and improved mood states). Some of the more frequently used techniques include:

- **progressive muscle relaxation** – tightening and relaxing specific muscles
- **autogenic relaxation** – technique of focusing on producing self-induced heavy and warm sensations within specific muscle groups
- **imagery** – using the imagination to create a vivid scene in the mind, promoting feelings of comfort and relaxation
- **breathing drills** – breathing deeply to produce a state of relaxation.

Developing performer self-monitoring programmes is an effective method of guarding against overtraining, concerns with regular sleep patterns, illness or injury. Section 7 examines ways in which your performers can monitor themselves on a regular basis and so provide an effective means of detecting signs of illness, injury or overtraining.

The next activity requires you to take the process of adaptation and the Principles of Training into account when designing a programme of training for one training component. When you plan a training programme in terms of volume and intensity, it is essential to plan recovery at the same time. It is important to choose the most relevant recovery technique for a particular training factor (eg endurance, strength or speed training).

Activity 14

1 Select one Performance Factor from your team or performer's profile.

2 Using the planner on the next page, plan a six-week training programme that you would use to develop this factor only. Disregard, for the present, the other demands on the performer's time and energy. Ensure the programme conforms to the Principles of Training given in this section.

3 Outline in detail the recovery periods planned in this programme.

Table 3: Six-week training programme

Week	Activity	Recovery
1		
2		
3		
4		
5		
6		

The ability to apply the Principles of Training in training programmes is central to the work of the coach in any sport. The process you have completed in this exercise should be repeated for all the Performance Factors.

Part B – Section 6 – will help you to merge the different components of the Performance Factors into quality training programmes.

It is important that the overall training load does not exceed the capabilities of your performer. So you must be very aware of the age and stage of young performers, in terms of what they need to develop, what they can develop and by how much. In some sports, there is a real danger of overtraining young performers. When moving young performers from one microcycle (see Section 6) to the next, it is important to keep the increment in training load to less than 20%. Building athletic performance slowly and progressively is essential. The next section deals with the potential for overtraining and makes suggestions for how it can be avoided through careful planning and monitoring.

Overtraining

Figure 10 shows how the human body adapts to training through the process of overcompensation. However, it is important that you understand how poor planning, a lack of understanding of growth and development issues in young performers and a lack of understanding of the Principles of Training can all lead to overtraining.

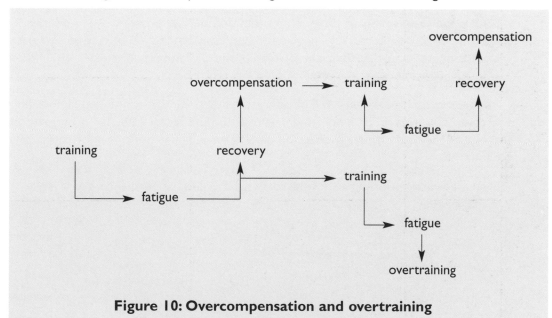

Figure 10: Overcompensation and overtraining

We have already noted that if the performer trains again before full recovery, overcompensation does not happen. Instead, overtraining occurs, the quality of performance is reduced and adaptation does not take place.

Overtraining is considered to be a temporary imbalance between training and recovery, most easily noticed as fatigue that does not disappear with normal levels of rest. As a result, performance deteriorates because the performer experiences **increasing** difficulty in recovering between training sessions. Overtraining is characterised by a complex range of the following physical and mental signs and symptoms, some or all of which may present themselves:

- reduced performance in training and/or competition
- loss of weight
- loss of appetite
- muscle soreness/tenderness
- increased susceptibility to colds
- lack of motivation for intensive training
- sleeping difficulty
- slow recovery from training
- general irritability
- increased heart rate during activity
- increased resting heart rate.

Recognising the occurrence of some or all of these symptoms in your performers should alert you to the possibility of overtraining. It is important that you seek expert advice[1] on the diagnosis in order to subsequently manage the situation if you are concerned.

The difficulty, of course, is that every individual is unique and work intensities and recovery periods for one performer will not necessarily be appropriate for another. This creates problems, especially for coaches who train squads and teams. It is inappropriate to develop team or squad programmes that do not take account of individual differences. To counteract this problem, many team coaches stream their performers into different groups. Athletics or swimming squad members may work on different training programmes at the same time in adjacent lanes.

In addition, each performer will be affected by different environmental factors (eg social pressures, work, school, employment, family). If these factors are not managed correctly, they can have a detrimental effect on performance. There is more information on this in Section 5

Figure 11 illustrates the relationship between training, performance and lifestyle management.

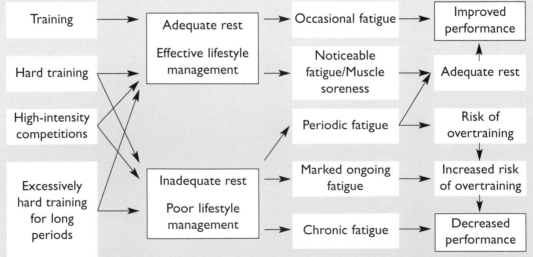

Figure 11: Interrelationships between training, fatigue, overtraining and lifestyle (adapted from Martin and Coe[2])

[1] If you require further advice on the diagnosis and treatment of overtraining syndrome, you should contact the British Association of Sport and Exercise Medicine (BASEM), BASEM Central Office, 15 Hawthorne Avenue, Norton, Doncaster DN6 9HR (tel: 01302-709 342, email: basemcentral@basem.co.uk).

[2] Martin, D.E. and Coe, P.N. (1992) *Training Distance Runners: the art and science of optimal training.* Champaign, IL: Leisure Press, p264 (out of print).

4.3 Recap and What Next?

It should be very clear that:

- coaches need to understand the Principles of Training
- the Principles of Training are important and a fundamental in the design of any training programme
- recovery is a very important consideration in planning training programmes
- it is not only excessive training loads that lead to overtraining; the training programme may well be within your performers' limits, but the sum of all the other demands on them as individuals (lifestyle etc) can so increase the amount of energy needed that, in the end, the performer is overwhelmed
- it is important to monitor your performers and encourage them to monitor themselves for overtraining or chronic fatigue. Some useful procedures are outlined in Section 5.

Further reading

For further information on some of the topics covered in this section, the following books will prove useful. Both these resources are available from Coachwise 1st4sport (0113-201 5555 or www.1st4sport.com).

Dick, F.W. (2007) *Sports Training Principles*. 5th edition. London, A & C Black. ISBN: 978-0713682-78-6.

sports coach UK (2002) *Physiology and Performance*. 3rd edition. Leeds: Coachwise Business Solutions/The National Coaching Foundation. ISBN: 978-947850-24-4.

© Alan Edwards

Section 5

Lifestyle Management

5.0 What this Section is About

With so much training and recovery to fit into the programme, it is very clear that sport can dominate a performer's life. You know from experience that many performers are completely focused on their goals for their sport, almost to the exclusion of everything else. You also know that such one-dimensional lifestyles are not in the long-term interest of the performers. On the other hand, you will probably have encountered some very talented performers who find it difficult to commit the time to training that their talent requires, and so never fulfil their potential. How do you strike the right balance between these two extremes?

Your task, as a coach, is to help your performers manage the areas of their life over which you have no control, so that their life is full and balanced, without affecting their sporting performance.

This applies equally to coaches of teams and individual performers.

You will know that the roles undertaken by coaches are many – being a successful and caring coach extends the role *of training performers for competition* to include that of counsellor, friend and lifestyle manager. These are important roles for a coach, because performance in competition and training cannot be isolated from the rest of a performer's life.

In this section, you will also look at how you might integrate your performers' sporting goals more effectively into their lifestyles.

By the end of this section, you should be able to:

• help your performers to balance their sporting commitments with other lifestyle commitments

• integrate lifestyle considerations into your planning

• adjust the plan when unexpected events occur.

5.1 Lifestyle Management

Time and energy are both limited resources. The time and energy available to a performer must be maximised so that training programmes are effective and so performance in competition is maximised. There are many demands on the time and energy of a performer, from the requirements of training and from other commitments outside the sport (school or work commitments, commitments in other sports, family commitments and so on). The effective management of these resources by the performers and the coach will often feel like walking a tightrope. The consequences of a misjudgement can be severe. Lifestyle management is about balancing the demands on a performer's time and energy. It is integral to the coach's task. *For young performers, the Junior Athlete Education programme, which is part of the Gifted and Talented programme, can help them to develop and understand how they can help themselves[1].*

Participation in performance-level sport almost always requires a sacrifice or even disruption in some other area of life (often the social life or career). This can be difficult for many performers, but a well-managed lifestyle can help to minimise the disruption. Lifestyle management is an area in which coaches are often wary, but a common cause of performers dropping out of sport, or failing to reach their potential, is lack of fulfilment in another area of life. This section will help you to help your performers to balance training programmes with the other aspects of their lives.

The following information and discussion might seem more relevant to coaches in individual sports than team sports. However, team coaches are also coaches of individuals and they have the added task of blending these individuals into a cohesive team. A team coach must design training programmes to meet the needs of the team, but in developing and implementing them, the coach needs to be sympathetic to the individuals within the team. Every individual will face similar but unique problems in balancing home life, work, education and other issues with his or her commitment to sport. Some individuals can find this more difficult than others. In a team sport, morale and team spirit can be adversely affected if the same commitment is not seen to be given by all players. The coach must not avoid this problem. It can contribute significantly – positively and negatively – to performance.

Non-training Stress

We have already discussed the fact that training for sport requires performers to subject themselves to specific stresses, and that the body adapts and becomes more effective at coping with such stress. Adaptation to any form of stress requires energy, which is a limited resource for everybody, including performers. However, there are many sources of stress other than those imposed in training. All these sources of non-training stress also demand energy. The more stress imposed by factors external to training, the less energy your performers will have available to cope with the stresses imposed in training.

[1] For more information on the Junior Athlete Education programme, see
www.youthsporttrust.org/subpage/gifted-and-talented/index.htm

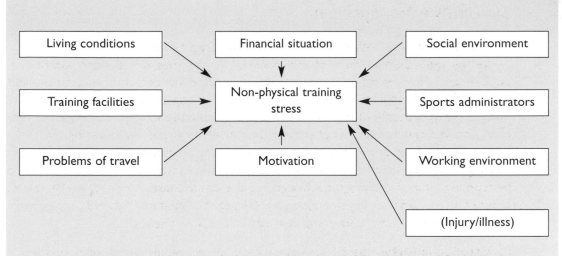

Figure 12: Factors that contribute to non-training stress

Performers will often need help to manage all the conflicting commitments in their lives. This is where your role as friend and counsellor can be most effective. Often, performers are so involved in the day-to-day hustle that they have never stopped to look at the 'big picture'. An objective examination of their lifestyle can provide them with the insight to reassess their priorities and the allocation of their time. You can be the stimulus for this.

Two tools will be of particular help to you in this regard: the **lifestyle audit** and the **lifestyle progress chart**[1]. The former is a snapshot of the current commitments of performers, and the amount of time devoted to them. The latter is a map of future commitments, in which you endeavour to anticipate and account for future disruptions to performers' training programme.

Lifestyle audit

To gain maximum benefit from your performers' energy, the use of their time must be planned and rationalised. The lifestyle audit is a tool which will help you and your performers to assess current commitments and priorities. You will then be able to address any disparities in the allocation of time to the different areas of their lives.

Activity 15

Select a performer who you work with and, in conversation with him or her, complete the following tasks:

1 Select the headings which best describe the important areas in the performer's lifestyle from the following list (add other headings if necessary):

Work   Education   Family

Social   Sport   Recreation/leisure

Other

---

[1] Coaches face similar time-management problems to performers. You may find it useful to use these tools to assess your own lifestyle.

2 In the following table, fill in each box with the amount of time (in hours) devoted to each area of life. Use an average week as an example.

	Mon	Tues	Wed	Thurs	Fri	Sat	Sun
Morning							
Afternoon							
Evening							

3 Total the time spent on each area of life, per week:

Work .... hrs

Education .... hrs

Family .... hrs

Social .... hrs

Sport .... hrs

Recreation .... hrs

Other .... hrs

.... hrs

4 Ask your performer to reflect on how this breakdown reflects his or her priorities. Assess how you could reallocate time to reflect them more accurately.

You know that sporting activity is a significant part of your performer's life and indeed of your own. Did you realise how significant? When balanced against the time demands of other commitments external to sport – for example, family, study, relationships – the commitment can be seen clearly.

The lifestyle progress chart

Performers' lifestyles are not static and their priorities are likely to change over time, and as they grow older. It is important to know their current non-training stresses, but you must also know how these are likely to alter in the future. With this knowledge, you can be sure that the programmes you develop have 'built-in' plans for the future and that present plans are realistic. If the programmes are unrealistic, you will encounter problems with burnout, lack of motivation and the erosion of self-confidence. *The lifestyle progress chart* can help to ensure your current and future programmes are realistic.

A lifestyle chart is divided into two parts – one environmental (focusing on family, education and career) and one sport-specific. It could be based on a four-year cycle culminating in the Olympic Games, but it could equally be for one year or even a few months. In effect, this is a projection of the non-training stresses of the future, allowing the performer and coach to identify significant events in the performer's life, sporting and non-sporting.

Now is the time to start planning for an event that will have a significant effect on your performer's training or commitment to sport, not just before it happens. Events such as examinations, marriages, moving from school to college or from college to a job, job promotions or changes will have enormous impact on the energy that can be given to sport. Anticipate and deal with them in advance.

Construct a lifestyle progress chart (page 80) with a performer by completing the boxes in as much detail as possible. (You may like to alter the chart and make it more specific to your performer.)

Your performers do not operate in a social vacuum. At times, they will have the same significant problems that everyone faces in life. If you are working with young performers, these difficulties may centre around school, and relationships with friends and family. More mature performers will identify different problems and you will need to know about their lifestyle, work demands, perhaps finances, demands from home or social demands, such as personal relationships.

The lifestyle chart is a tool for monitoring progress and can highlight areas where expert help is required. Practitioners in a range of support services, including psychology, nutrition, education and career planning, could be consulted (if required) to give advice.

The two important points to remember with regard to lifestyle management are that:

• well-managed lifestyles are, in themselves, an enhancement to performance

• everyone involved in sport, including performers, should ensure that sport does not have a detrimental effect on the life of the individual.

If a performer's lifestyle is incorrectly managed, it can contribute to a state of increased fatigue and possibly lead to the development of overtraining. Overtraining was covered in more detail in Section 4.

Activity 16

1 Construct a lifestyle progress chart with a performer by completing the boxes in as much detail as possible.

2 You may like to alter the chart and make it more specific to your sport.

Qualifications Examinations	Career/Progress Ambition	Sporting Goals	Training Structure	Finances

5.2 Overcoming Unexpected Events

Regardless of how well you anticipate events, or how well you organise your time and your performer's time, unexpected events will occur which will require you to think again and to reprogramme your plans. Your performers may:

- become ill or injured
- make more rapid progress than expected
- fail exams and have to resit them
- undergo any number of personal, work, school or family-related events which were unforeseen and disrupt their training.

Your training facilities may close down unexpectedly due to weather or technical difficulties.

In any of these instances, your ability to adapt and successfully reprogramme the performer's/team's training will be the most significant factor in determining the impact of the event. When the unexpected occurs, you must **reassess and reprogramme**. This will often mean reducing training loads or eliminating certain components until the performer has recovered or the event has passed. The **whole programme** must be altered because of unexpected events.

It is tempting to ignore minor inconveniences to your plans and to carry on regardless. If the event is a minor one, which prevents participation in one component of training only, the performer is likely to be able to carry on with the remainder of the programme, and the effects might appear minimal. For example, a weight-room facility might be unavailable for three weeks. However, there is now some excess capacity in the performers' training programme which could be used in order to maximise training time. If it is not taken up by a revised programme, it will be swallowed by other parts of the performers' lives. When the performers return to weight training, it is likely that they will need to follow a remedial programme, which will again unbalance the programme. As a result, some other area which should be prioritised during this period will lose out. If the excess capacity was not used in the initial stages, performers will discover that they have lost more ground than was obvious at the start. No matter how small the event, the consequences are always likely to be greater than they appear at first.

Facilities planning

Until something goes wrong, coaches tend to take facilities for granted. When something does go awry, however, inadequate facilities can create havoc with your carefully planned programmes. Things do go wrong – for example, the weather may prevent performers from reaching the training venue, or facilities can break down or close unexpectedly. The time for contingency planning and the investigation of alternatives is now – not when it becomes a crisis. The next activity gives you the opportunity to reflect on solutions to potential, rather than actual, problems.

Activity 17

1   Consider how the facilities you use meet the needs of your programme. Identify any gaps that exist between the present facilities and your ideal requirements. These gaps may be in terms of time, access, quality, travel time and so on.

2   Take some time to identify possible solutions to these problems.

3   Now, draw up contingency plans in the event of facilities being unavailable due to unforeseen circumstances (weather, breakdowns and so on).

It is very difficult to prepare for unexpected events. However, by carrying out a simple investigation into the facilities you use, it may be possible to limit the damage caused by any unforeseen circumstances.

Rehabilitation of injury/illness

If a performer has missed a training unit/session, or even several days' training, it is probably possible to drop back into the programme with little change. However, where weeks or months have been missed, it is necessary to revise your plans. For example, if you have a performer who has suffered a serious injury and has missed a month's training, there will be a need to reset goals and redevelop your programme to meet the performer's needs.

Because of the principle of reversibility, a performer's level in all the Performance Factors – physical, technical, tactical and mental – will regress during a period of inactivity. For this reason, any components that may be maintained during a period of injury should be part of an adapted training programme. For example, a knee injury to a rugby player would not preclude mental-skills work or upper-body-strength work while the knee was recovering.

Remedial programmes

The injury will require a remedial programme which will be prescribed by a medical practitioner (eg sports doctor, sports physiotherapist). Always respect medical advice when dealing with remedial exercise, but ensure that the practitioner is experienced in the area of sports injury. In most cases, the remedial programme will begin up to one week after the injury. Remedial programmes to injured parts should be continued long after the treatment stops, and even after the return to full competition, to prevent a recurrence of the injury.

Rehabilitative training programmes always require a delicate balance between those components which may be maintained at the level they were at before injury, those which can be developed and the gradual rehabilitation of the components directly affected by the injury. The overall programme must be adapted throughout the period of injury and rehabilitation. Even when full recovery is achieved, the performer's training programme will not simply revert to the pre-injury programme, as some components will have progressed despite the injury, and some will require long-term rehabilitation programmes (as in the case of ankle-ligament damage). As progression from cycle to cycle in your initial programme is important, the same principle holds true for rehabilitation from injury or returning from illness. The temptation to accelerate the programme of recovery often leads to chronic problems, as the injury is likely to recur on premature return to competition or full training.

The mental and emotional components involved in coping with injury are very important. Your performer may experience feelings of low self-confidence and may feel quite helpless. It is essential at this stage to devote a lot of time to maintaining the performer's focus and increasing self-confidence. The coach must be innovative in adjusting the programme and present performers with positive images during any period of layoff – whatever the reason.

5.3 Recap and What Next?

This section has highlighted:

- the importance of lifestyle management for coach and performers – there is never enough time to do everything, but careful planning can maximise the time available, and ensure that both coach and performers have lifestyles that are balanced and so are conducive to long-term success and enjoyment of their sport
- the fact that, often, both coach and performers are so consumed with the present that longer-term and contingency-planning exercises are not considered
- that attention to both these issues can result in more effective programmes that can react quickly to adversity, and so increase the chances of overcoming unanticipated events.

For further information on some of the topics covered in this section, the following books will prove useful. The resource below is available from Coachwise 1st4sport (tel 0113-201 5555 or visit www.1st4sport.com).

Cabral, P. and Crisfield, P. (2005) *Motivation and Mental Toughness*. 2nd edition. Leeds: Coachwise Business Solutions/The National Coaching Foundation. ISBN: 978-902523-24-5.

Further reading

Kidman, L. and Hanrahan, S. (1997) *The Coaching Process*. Wellington: Dunmore Press. ISBN: 978-0-864694-61-4

If you require assistance from a sport scientist or sports medicine specialist, the following addresses will be useful:

British Association of Sport and Exercise Medicine (BASEM)
BASEM Central Office
15 Hawthorne Avenue
Norton
Doncaster DN6 9HR
Tel: 01302-709 342
Email: basemcentral@basem.co.uk
Website: www.basem.co.uk

British Association of Sport and Exercise Sciences (BASES)
Leeds Metropolitan University
Carnegie Faculty of Sport and Education
Fairfax Hall
Headingley Campus, Beckett Park
Leeds LS6 3QS
Tel: 0113-283 6162
Email: jbairstow@bases.org.uk
Website: www.bases.org.uk

Part B

Section 6

Planning Models

6.0 What this Section is About

As a coach, you now have the necessary information to construct high-quality training programmes for your performers and teams.

In Section 1, we outlined the different levels of planning that exist in the development of performers. The Performance Factors and components were discussed in Section 2. You decided which components of performance should be prioritised in your sport and, together with the performer/team, you set goals for those components in Section 3. The Principles of Training were discussed in detail in Section 4. And finally, the importance of considering lifestyle factors when planning was discussed in Section 5.

One of the coach's most difficult planning tasks is to fit all the individual components into a progressive and integrated plan, while making sure that the principles that affect training are taken into account.

This section will help you to develop plans for different time periods. These were discussed in Section 1 and are:

- 10–12 years (LTAD)
- four years (the Olympic cycle)
- 12 months (annual)
- 1–6/7 weeks (mesocycle)
- 2–7 days (microcycle)
- single sessions (which include training units).

By the end of this section, you should be able to:

• explain the different types and levels of training programmes that fit your sport

• construct a programme for your sport at each level

• begin the process of developing a 10–12-year LTAD plan for your sport

• explain how periodisation can make annual and quadrennial training programmes more efficient and effective

• divide your annual programme into appropriate training phases for your sport

• outline the training content of each one of these phases

• explain the content of individual sessions

• explain the principles for making optimal use of available training time.

6.1 10–12-year Plans (LTAD)

The information given on page 6 in Section 1 on long-term plans is important for the following activity. It would help to revise this before you begin Activity 18.

Activity 18

From your perspective as a coach, make notes of what you notice about the charts on the following pages. Then try to give your reasons for the differences and similarities that exist between them.

1 Issues of note in the charts:

2 Differences between the charts:

3 Similarities between the charts:

**Figure 13: LTAD Plans
Paddlesport**

	FOUNDATION PHASE		PERFORMANCE PHASE			RECREATION PHASE
	FUNdamentals Male: 5–10 years of age Female: 4–9 years of age	**Paddlesport Start and Development** Male: 8–14 years of age Female: 7–13 years of age	**Training to Train** Male: 11–17 years of age Female: 10–15 years of age	**Training to Perform** Male: 14–21 years of age Female: 12–20 years of age	**Training to Excel** Male: 17 years of age Female: 15 years of age	**Recreation** Personal choice
	Focus on: • Fun! • Learning to move.	*Focus on:* • Fun! • Introducing and developing paddlesport skills.	*Focus on:* • Developing physiological and technical abilities.	*Focus on:* • Optimising physiological and technical skills.	*Focus on:* • Producing high-level performances.	*Focus on:* • Individual needs.
	This stage is important for developing: • agility, balance and coordination • movement skills • speed work:rest ratio of 1:5 • joint stability • strength through own body weight • swimming and water skills • confidence in movement and in water • at least 3 other sports.	This stage is important for developing: • motor-skill learning in flat and moving water • endurance • flexibility and joint stability • speed work:rest ratio of 1:5 • strength using own body weight • 2–3 other sports.	This stage is important for developing: • aerobic conditioning • speed work:rest ratio of 1:4 • strength (towards end of stage) • flexibility and joint stability • discipline-specific skills • other sports, as appropriate • basic mental skills • use and understanding of specific tactics. Be aware of growth spurt.	This stage is important for developing: • speed work:rest ratio of 1:4 • maximum strength and power • endurance • flexibility and joint stability • discipline-specific skills • consistency of performance • mental skills • effective use of tactics.	This stage is important for meeting the needs of the schedule, working on: • speed work:rest ratio of 1:4 • strength • flexibility and joint stability • endurance • advanced mental skills • individual programmes to work on specific areas as necessary.	This stage is important for developing or maintaining: • injury-free fitness • injury-free technical skills • physiological, mental, technical and tactical skills that are appropriate to personal needs and goals • effective goal-setting skills.
	Volume/intensity of training: • High volume • Low intensity.	Volume/intensity of training: • According to growth – likely to be high volume with increasing intensity.	Volume/intensity of training: • According to growth – likely to be low volume with increasing intensity.	Volume/intensity of training: • High volume with increasing intensity.	Volume/intensity of training: • High volume • High intensity.	Volume/intensity of training: • To suit individual but likely to be low volume with medium intensity.

Number and length of sessions per week: • 4–6 sessions of physical activity • 1 water session (In total, there should be 1 water session to every 3 other sports sessions.) 30–60-minute sessions.	**Number and length of sessions per week:** • 3 hours of paddling in total • 3 hours of other sports • Sessions in different types of craft. 30–90-minute sessions.	**Number and length of sessions per week:** • 3–8 paddling sessions. • Appropriate land-based training sessions. 45–120-minute sessions.	**Number and length of sessions per week:** • 7–14 specific training sessions. • Appropriate land-based training. 45–120-minute sessions.	**Number and length of sessions per week:** • Individualised. 45–120-minute sessions.	**Number and length of sessions:** • Individualised to suit lifestyle.
Type of events: • Multi-sports festivals/camps that are informal and fun.	**Type of events:** • Events providing a wide range of discipline experience.	**Type of events based on:** • Specialisation in discipline-specific events.	**Type of events based on:** • Double/triple periodisation based around event calendar.	**Type of events based on:** • Double/triple/ multiple periodisation • Individual event planning.	**Type of events based on:** • Individual choice.
Number of events: • Unlimited.	**Number of events based on:** • Training 75% • Performing 25%.	**Number of events based on:** • Training 75% • Performing 25%.	**Number of events based on:** • Training 50% • Performing 50%.	**Number of events based on:** • Training 50% • Performing 50%.	**Number of events:** • Depends on individual choice.
Venues: • Clubs • Centres • Schools.	**Venues:** Different venues for different types of paddling, but include: • Clubs • Centres • Schools.	**Venues:** • Clubs • Squads.	**Venues:** • Clubs • Squads.	**Venues:** • Clubs • Squads.	**Venues:** • Individual choice • Clubs • Outdoor centres.
Coaches: • Club • Centre • Teachers.	**Coaches:** • Club • Centre • Teachers.	**Coaches:** • Club • Squad • Regional • Personal.	**Coaches:** • Club • Squad • Personal.	**Coaches:** • Club • Squad • Personal.	**Coaches:** • Club • Personal.

© The National Coaching Foundation and The British Canoe Union, 2006

Judo

FUNdamentals 6–10 years of age	Pre-start Learning to train Male: 9–12 years Female: 8–11 years	Start Training to train Male: 12–18 years Female: 11–15 years	Potential Training to compete Male: 16–25 years Female: 15–23 years	Performance Training to win Ages 20+	Recreation Individual choice
This stage is important for learning the FUNdamental movement skills of: • agility, balance and coordination • running, throwing, jumping and catching • speed • strength through own body weight • learning to work with others • other sports.	This stage is important for learning the FUNdamental sports skills of: • motor skills – more judo skills • endurance • flexibility • strength through own body weight • mental preparation (introduction) • at least 3 other sports. Be aware of biological readiness.	This stage is important for building fitness and learning judo skills, concentrating on: • aerobic conditioning • speed • strength (towards end of stage) • flexibility • mental preparation (development) • tactical preparation • at least 1–2 other sports. Be aware of biological readiness.	This stage is important for refining the fitness and judo skills of: • speed • strength • power • plyometric training • endurance • advanced judo skills • high-level tactical concepts • high-quality decision making • mental preparation (optimisation).	This stage is important for maximising competitive performance through: • individual-specific judo training • technical and tactical preparation • specific speed training • individual strength work • endurance training • advanced mental-skills development.	This stage is important for remaining involved in judo and physical activity.
Volume/intensity of training: • High volume • Low intensity.	Volume/intensity of training: • According to growth, but likely to be high volume with increasing intensity.	Volume/intensity of training: • According to growth, but likely to be lower volume with increasing intensity.	Volume/intensity of training: • High volume • Increasing intensity.	Volume/intensity of training: • High volume • High intensity.	Volume/intensity of training: • Volume and intensity to suit individual.
Number and length of sessions per week: • 1–2 sessions of judo (45–60 mins) • 4–5 sessions of physical activity.	Number and length of sessions per week: • 2–3 sessions of judo (45–75 mins) • 3–4 sessions of general activity.	Number and length of sessions per week: • 5–7 sessions of judo (45–90 mins) • 3–4 sessions of general activity or judo conditioning.	Number and length of sessions per week: • 5–9 sessions of judo (60–90 mins) • 5–6 sessions of judo conditioning.	Number and length of sessions per week: • 5–12 sessions of judo (60–120 mins) • 4–6 sessions of judo conditioning.	Number and length of sessions per week: • Mixture of judo/physical activity to suit personal needs.

Type/amount of competition: • Fun events • Judo festivals.	**Type/amount of competition:** • Club events • Mini-mon • Area cadet. 2–4 competitions per year.	**Type/amount of competition:** • Club events • Area cadet • National cadet • International cadet. 4–8 competitions per year.	**Type/amount of competition:** • National junior/senior • International junior/senior. 8–12 competitions per year.	**Type/amount of competition:** • National junior/senior • International junior/senior. Peaking for major championships and selection events	**Type/amount of competition:** • National Masters • International Masters.
Number of gradings (per year): • 2–3 non-competitive junior gradings.	**Number of gradings (per year):** • 2–3 non-competitive junior gradings • Introduction to competitive gradings for more experienced players.	**Number of gradings (per year):** • 2–3 competitive junior/senior gradings.	**Number of gradings (per year):** • 2–4 competitive senior gradings.	**Number of gradings (per year):** • 2–4 competitive senior gradings.	**Number of gradings (per year):** • Own choice.
Playing venues: • School • Club.	**Training venues:** • School • Club.	**Training venues:** • School • Club • Regional training centre • National training centre.	**Training venues:** • Club • High-performance regional training centre • National training centre.	**Training venues:** • Club • High-performance regional training centre • National training centre.	**Training venues:** • Club • Regional Masters • National Masters.
Coaches: • Level 2 assisted by Level 1.	**Coaches:** • Level 2 assisted by Level 1.	**Coaches:** • Level 2–3.	**Coaches:** • Level 2–4.	**Coaches:** • Level 2–5.	**Coaches:** • Those with relevant experience and education.

© The National Coaching Foundation and The British Judo Association, 2006

• *You will probably have noticed that the Performance Factors are on both charts and that they have similar components at each age and stage. The ages for boys and girls at the same stage are different. Both charts have six stages of development and the stages overlap each other.*

• *The major differences between these charts are the names of the ages and stages, but the Windows of Trainability (Opportunity) referred to in Section I in each are similar. This is because growth and development in children is the same, whatever the sport. The ages given are chronological and no indication of developmental (biological) age is given on these long-term and, therefore, 'general' plans.*

• *You will also have noticed that the amount of periodisation increases progressively as the performer moves through the stages of LTAD. Thus, Training to Win will have a much greater implementation of periodisation than Training to Train.*

4 Using what you know of LTAD in your own sport, try to complete as many sections as possible of the blank LTAD plan in Appendix A. You will need to know whether your sport is an early or late specialisation sport. You may need to ask your governing body of sport for some guidance with this exercise and so will need time to complete the chart. At this time, use it as a work in progress.

6.2 Four-year Plans – the Olympic Cycle

Activity 19

Make some notes below on what sort of plan you would expect an Olympic sport to use and how it could be constructed. You will need to consider goal setting and competition for each of the four years, as well as ensuring that training is progressive over the time frame. Each year's programme should build on the year before and prepare for the next.

Now turn over.

You might have found making these notes easier if your sport is an Olympic sport, but the principal issue is that the plan is based on a progressive set of annual plans. Each annual plan can be thought of as a macrocycle (see 6.3 below).

6.3 Annual Planning – Periodisation

Developing annual plans can be daunting. The activities that follow will take you through the principles of doing so and thus help you to develop an actual plan (from the blank plan in Appendix A), at the end of this section.

Activity 20

1 What do you notice in terms of differences between the two annual plans on the following pages?

2 What are the contrasts between them and the LTAD charts?

Annual Plan

Month	Week	Training phases Macro	Meso	Competition	Intensity 1–5	Peaking	Testing	Components	Goals
June	6th	General prep	I(a)		2		T	Base strength aerobic base individual	Individual aerobic/strength goals
June	13th		I(a)		2				
June	20th		I(b)		3				
June	27th				3				
July	4th				3				
July	11th		I(b)		3		T		
July	18th	Spec prep	II(a)		4			Power speed	Achieve set-piece stability; Develop defensive game plan; Develop offensive game plan
July	25th				4				
August	1st				4				
August	8th				4				
August	15th		II(b)	Challenge (H)	5	★		Tech anaer	
August	22nd			Challenge (H)	5				
August	29th			Challenge (A)	5				
September	5th	Competition	III	League 1 (H)	5			Technical	Develop match patterns; 1 possession; 2 territorial
September	12th			League 2 (A)	5				
September	19th			League 3 (H)	5				
September	26th			League 4 (A)	3				
October	3rd			Challenge (H)	3				
October	10th			League 5 (H)	4				
October	17th			League 6 (A)	5	★			
October	24th			League 7 (H)	5				
November	31st	Rec	IV	Off	2			Tech	Review and develop match Patterns; Review individual fitness levels
November	7th			Cup (local)	2				
November	14th	Prep (spec)	V(a)	Cup (local)	3			End base	
November	21st			Cup (local)	3				
November	28th			Cup (local)	3				
December	3rd			Cup/Challenge	3		T		
December	12th		V(b)	League 8 (A)	4			Ana ero bic	
December	19th			Cup/Challenge	4				
December	26th			Challenge	5	★			
January	2nd	Competition		League 9 (A)	5			Technical	Develop advanced patterns
January	9th		VI	League 10 (H)	5				
January	16th			Cup/Challenge	5				
January	23rd			League 11 (H)	3				
January	30th			League 12 (A)	3				
February	6th		VII	League 13 (H)	4				
February	13th			League 14 (A)	5	★			
February	20th			League 15 (H)	5				
February	27th			League 16 (A)	5				
March	6th		VIII	Cup RD 1	5				
March	13th			Challenge	5				
March	20th			Cup RD 2	5				
March	27th			Challenge					
April	3rd			Cup RD 3					
April	10th			Challenge					
April	17th								
April	24th								
May	1st	Recovery	IX						
May	8th								
May	13th								
May	22nd								
May	29th								

Figure 14: Annual plan for a rugby union club side

Month	January				February				March					April					May					June				July				August				September				October					November					December		
Week	1	2	3	4	5	6	7	8	9	10	11	12	13	14	15	16	17	18	19	20	21	22	23	24	25	26	27	28	29	30	31	32	33	34	35	36	37	38	39	40	41	42	43	44	45	46	47	48	49	50	51	52
Comp phase + Training phase macro	recov →		preparation →						pre-comp **1**			comp r → **1**					prep **1** →			p c **2**		comp r **2** →		prep →				pre-comp **3**			comp **3**				recovery ↑↓				prep					pre-comp **4**		comp **4**	p c		comp		
Training phase meso	18		1						2			3					4		5		6	7	8	9				10			11					12				13					14		15	16		17		
Intensity 1-5			2	2	3	3	4	4	5	3	3						3	3	4		4			4	4	4	4	5	4											2	3	3	4	5	4			4			
Volume 1-5			5	5	4	5	4	4	3	4	3						5	5	4		3			4	5	5	4	3	3											5	5	4	4	4	3	3		3			
Peaking												5	8	8	9						8	9									5	7	8	9	9											5	7		7	8	9
Testing	X																	X																				X														

Goals				
Physical	improve all capacities esp. strength and speed	speed	maintain	
Technical	rkt head speed on slice return of serve loading/kinetic chain		approach shot	
Tactical	patterns for serve/return	serve/return	patterns	baseline play
Mental	positive approach	concentration routines	concentration routines	manage mistakes

Figure 15: Annual plan for a tennis player

You will probably have noticed that the level of training and competition detail has increased in both of these plans. The months of the year are clearly defined as being periods of either training, competition or rest/transition.

You will also have noticed that the number of competition periods is greater for tennis than it is for rugby union. You will have noticed that testing is built in.

As a coach, you may be familiar with the annual planning process that divides the performer's/team's programme into separate training, competition and recovery/transition periods, each with different goals and training methods. These periods are designed to maximise gains in the different Performance Factors. This process of planning is called **periodisation**.

© Alan Edwards

We have discussed already that each sport has its own characteristics. Periodisation will also be highly sport-specific. For team sports, periodisation is usually quite straightforward and is based on that team's goals. However, in individual sports, apart from the sport's characteristics, what works for one performer may not work for another, so, to some extent, periodisation must also be individual-specific. One reason is because different performers follow different competitive schedules. We have highlighted before that the whole point of training is to *compete* at a higher and more proficient level. So it follows that if competitive schedules are different, so are periodisation plans.

If you are working with young performers who are at different developmental (biological) ages, you will have to be very specific in your planning both to maximise the Windows of Trainability (Opportunity) and minimise the risk of injury. There is, therefore, no single plan that you can apply to all your performers. You must work through the principles of periodisation and apply them to your sport and to each performer and team with whom you work.

That said, the *principles* which govern periodisation are common to all sports, though, in some cases, the terminology may be used in slightly different ways. We will now work through the principles of periodisation, starting at the simplest situation and building your understanding from there. The initial activities may or may not seem relevant to you, but they are a necessary stepping stone to the later parts of this section, so please ensure you understand each one before moving on.

The first principle is to divide the year into different periods of *training, competition and rest/transition*. These are then subdivided into three levels of training cycles. These cycles build on each other during the year to form the periodised plan. They are known as:

• macrocycles

• mesocycles

• microcycles.

A **macrocycle** is a phase of considerable length, aimed at achieving peak performance in competition. It includes the training, competition and rest/transition periods, so in the rugby union plan, there are two macrocycles. In the annual plans on the previous pages, you will notice the macrocycle underneath the date column. The length of the macrocycle will vary with the sport and depend on the number of competition peaks for that sport. In team sports, the macrocycles usually correspond to the annual season. In the tennis plan, however, you will notice that there are four macrocycles, because competitions take place throughout the year.

In addition, macrocycles can be planned over longer phases or world cups and other major competitions, such as Olympic and Commonwealth Games, thus forming part of quadrennial plans (see 6.2).

Mesocycles are subdivisions of macrocycles, usually with a duration of 1–6/7 weeks. In the rugby union plan, you will notice there are nine mesocycles, three of which are subdivided again into two. Each mesocycle has a specific objective, linked to the objectives of the mesocycles preceding and following it, but, in turn, being part of the macrocycle.

Microcycles are usually 2–7 days in duration and several of them build into a mesocycle. They contain detailed information regarding the intensity, volume, content and sequence of all the individual training sessions.

Planning macrocycles

A macrocycle is a phase of training, competition and recovery/transition in which a team or performer aims to train for peak performance in competition. The length and intensity of the competitive peak will vary according to the sport and the stage of development of the performer/team. Young performers should have fewer macrocycles, irrespective of their sport, although the number (in sports with several competitive peaks during a year) could increase to three or four as they mature. In order to produce a peak performance, each macrocycle must be carefully structured and contain the three basic elements of:

• preparation

• competition

• recovery/transition.

The objectives of each of these periods are as follows:

Preparation: to prepare fully for the demands of competition. Most of the gains in the physical, technical, tactical and mental areas will be made in this period.

Competition: to maintain the gains of the preparation period and to bring every aspect of performance to a peak in major competitions.

Recovery/transition: to recuperate from the demands of competition, mentally and physically, and move to a higher level of performance in the next macrocycle.

This pattern of preparation, competition and recovery/transition is a recurring one. A periodised plan must ensure that a competitive period is followed by one of recovery/transition.

The training programmes of all performers will vary considerably from one macrocycle to the next in content and focus. Your first task is to divide your programme into the appropriate number of macrocycles for your sport. The following information will help you to make sure you do this in the most effective way.

The division of the programme is dependent on two important factors:

• the competitive structure of the sport
• the priorities of the performer.

For many performers and many sports, the annual competitive year is the realistic planning tool. This means that the competitive year is the macrocycle and is divided into the three periods outlined above. This assumes that there is *at least* one time in the year when the performers or team will want to compete at their optimal performance level. Remember again – the point of training is to compete at a higher level. Olympic sports obviously require optimal performance at longer intervals of four years. In these cases, coaches know that preparation may actually last for two years or more.

In contrast to the Olympic sports, performers in football and tennis have competitions for 30 weeks or more. For football players, it is not possible to maintain a peak of performance for a full season of competition. Players will aim to reach a plateau of performance that will be slightly below peak performance, and to maintain this plateau for as long as possible. The principles that produce that plateau are the same as those that produce a peak. In tennis, the 30+ weeks of competition are split into three or four periods of time and players plan their year to peak in each of these periods.

Remember, though, that, in football, players will sometimes aim to reach a higher peak of performance for very important competitions. The preparation and recovery associated with peaking may make it difficult to play consistently in competitions before and after the peak. Many coaches will prioritise competitions during a season. This allows them to use the less important competitions as preparation for the peak. They also use a 'pool' of players that they can rotate and so maintain peak team performance.

Try the next activity. It may be useful to bear a particular performer or team in mind as you complete it.

Activity 21

1 Study the example below which shows the preparation period, the competition period and the recovery period for a county netball player in the UK.

Jan	Feb	Mar	Apr	May	Jun	Jul	Aug	Sept	Oct	Nov	Dec
1	2	3	4	5	6	7	8	9	10	11	12
Comp				Rec		Prep			Comp		

Seasonal periodisation for netball

2 On the sample planner below, mark in the competitive period, preparation period and recovery period for your sport in the first free row.

Jan	Feb	Mar	Apr	May	Jun	Jul	Aug	Sept	Oct	Nov	Dec
1	2	3	4	5	6	7	8	9	10	11	12

3 Consider your own squad or a particular individual. In the second free row, mark in the *major* competitive events, using an asterisk. This will help you to be more detailed in your planning at a later stage.

© Alan Edwards

This may have been quite straightforward or you may have found it difficult, depending on your previous knowledge and your sport. If your sport is one which requires a continuous level of performance over a season, such as netball or rugby, your competitive period will have been quite lengthy. If, on the other hand, your competitive season is very focused on one competition, with other competitions merely used to build to that climax, the competitive period may have been quite short.

The important times of competition are now quite well established for most sports. If your sport requires a number of different competitive peaks in one season, you may have found the exercise more difficult, though the same basic principles apply. The following information will help you to apply these principles to more detailed plans.

Double periodisation

In Activity 21, an example of a typical single periodised year was shown. For a netball team, this is quite appropriate, as the competitive period is quite long and there is no break of significance. In other sports, however, such as swimming, the sport may require the performer to peak for two major competitions per year. In this case, your planning will need to have a double periodisation. Figure 16 shows an example of a yearly training cycle for a double periodised year for distance swimming and a quadruple one for tennis.

Swimming

Sept	Oct	Nov	Dec	Jan	Feb	Mar	Apr	May	Jun	Jul	Aug
1	2	3	4	5	6	7	8	9	10	11	12
Preparation		Competition			R	Preparation			Competition		R

Tennis

Sept	Oct	Nov	Dec	Jan	Feb	Mar	Apr	May	Jun	Jul	Aug
1	2	3	4	5	6	7	8	9	10	11	12
R/T	Comp	R/T	Prep	Comp	R/T	Prep	Competition		R/T	Prep	Comp

Figure 16: An example of a double periodised year in distance swimming and a quadruple year for tennis

Thus, periodisation is essentially sequential – the different periods follow each other. For example, competition should always be followed by recovery/transition. If the sequence is not followed, it is difficult for the performer to improve the Performance Factors in a logical and balanced way, and so, ultimately, performance will not be maximised.

The preparation phase

In most sports, the period of preparation is usually subdivided into two – a general phase and a specific phase. The length **of each** will vary depending on the age of the performer. With younger performers, it will be longer. Some sports call the preparation phase the *pre-season phase* and, in others, the specific preparation phase is called the *pre-competitive phase*.

General preparatory phase (GPP)

In the general phase, the emphasis is normally on general physical conditioning and general skill (technical) training. It is characterised by a large quantity of training at low intensities – high volume, low intensity work.

The focus may be on physical training (depending on the performers' developmental age), but it is also a good time for working on technique, tactical development and applying mental skills to different situations. Practical experience in many sports has shown that performance in competition is substantially determined by the training achieved in the first stage of the preparatory phase. If the training load is increased too much in the general phase, an inability to sustain performance and peak during the competitive phase may result.

The content of the general phase for adult performers would normally include the components listed below. This content would be modified for young performers according to their developmental age. As a coach, you will know the key elements of physical development that are important at each age and stage:

- **Aerobic fitness training** provides the foundation of training and is the springboard for more intensive activity. Typical activities might include long continuous runs, fartlek training (mixed-pace runs), easy-paced interval training and circuit work.

- **Strength training** is intended to develop a solid base from which to work. It will concentrate on improving strength in the major muscle groups and those specifically required for your sport. Preparation is the time for eliminating individual deficiencies and strengthening weaknesses (eg speed, explosive leg power, upper-body strength). Core strength training would also be important.

- **Muscular endurance training** (if this is a key quality in your sport). Training in the preparation phase should include a variety of speed and endurance training sessions.

- Time for working on individual **technical skills** within your sport. This should include the improvement and/or maintenance of existing technique and the learning of new skills. It may be possible to combine technical sessions with fitness sessions.

- **Mental skills training** should be a key component of this phase. This is the time for establishing the base skills in areas such as concentration and relaxation. The skills need to be developed in this phase before they can be applied in competition.

As a coach, try to think about the types of training you would do with young performers of 10–12 years of age or those of 15–16 years of age. What factors would help you to determine the components you would plan into your programme?

Specific preparatory phase (SPP) (called the pre-competitive phase [PCP] in some sports)

The specific phase of preparation for adult performers is characterised by an increased intensity and specialisation of training – the training becomes more competition-specific. The specific phase is a transition between the general preparatory phase and the early competition phase. Skills are honed to a fine edge, so they can be performed under the pressures of competition. Simulated competition exercises may be used to prepare performers for the competitive situation. The content of the specific phase would normally include the following:

- **Technical/tactical** work that focuses on individual skills and unit, team and tactical training, if appropriate. For example, a rugby team may decide to concentrate on scrummaging in this phase and could combine tactics and technique with power training.

- **Physical training** that is sport-specific (eg marathon runners should concentrate on being able to repeat distances at race pace). High-intensity training should be planned to build up to the important competitions. This is complicated in some sports (eg team games), in which performers are expected to perform to high levels over several weeks or even months. Weekly training must be designed to prepare performers to peak regularly on game days. In other sports (eg track and field athletics or swimming), performers typically train to peak for major competitions. The build-up is therefore more gradual and early-season competitions are used for training purposes.

- **Mental skills training** that now begins to be more specific and should be integrated into each training session. This phase provides the opportunity to put into practice some of the mental skills developed in the general preparatory phases. You may begin to encourage performers to monitor their own feelings and moods. Specific pre-competition routines need to be established; coping strategies must be decided on for dealing with unexpected events.

The SPP will be shorter than the GPP. As little as two or three weeks may be required to make the transition from training to competition intensity. The length of time this phase takes will depend on the individual, on the stage of development and the number of phases in the programme. Mature performers will be able to increase the intensity of their training smoothly, and will react rapidly to the change. Those at an earlier stage of development will require more time, possibly the same length of time as for the general preparation phase. Trial and error is the best method for determining optimal periodisation.

The concept of periodisation is derived for the most part from adult performance. From the point of view of working with young performers, the application of periodisation is more a reactive process – that is, the development of the individual child is the major consideration from two aspects. The first is to understand and use the Windows of Trainability (Opportunity) discussed in Section 1 (page 7). The second is that, once the performer has reached physical maturation, the programme should be periodised, based on both the assessed strengths and weaknesses of the performer and the demands of the sport.

Activity 22

Using the following table, divide your preparatory phase into both general and specific preparatory phases. Remember that you may only have one general preparatory phase, but may have more than one specific preparatory phase, depending on the structure of your sport.

Jan	Feb	Mar	Apr	May	Jun	Jul	Aug	Sep	Oct	Nov	Dec
1	2	3	4	5	6	7	8	9	10	11	12

The competition phase

The major objective during this phase is to compete consistently. Training intensity will rise, but training volume should decrease. The overall training load is reduced. Training must take account of the very specific demands and stresses of the forthcoming competition(s). This might mean using a prepared warm-up routine (physical and mental), a specific dietary pattern, planned periods of rest and relaxation between rounds, heats or matches, or training at the specific time of a future competition.

Mental and tactical preparation will take the place of physical and technical training. The emphasis will move to reinforcing the performer's/team's strengths. This helps to ensure that the performer's mind is ready for competition.

In team games, and others where performers must perform at a high level once or twice a week for extended periods, the coach has a delicate balance to maintain. Fitness levels will decline unless sufficient maintenance work is scheduled. On the other hand, an attempt to maintain fitness levels through high-volume training can lead to fatigue, which will affect performance in competition, and may ultimately develop into an overtraining situation. Careful manipulation of mesocycles and rating of competitions according to opposition quality may allow for training and recovery cycles to be built into seasonal schedules, even without a break in competition.

High volumes of training might be included in a maintenance mesocycle in mid-season. Large squads are a luxury that may allow the coach to rest players mid-season, as it becomes necessary, and so allow performers to maintain a high fitness level by playing fewer competitive fixtures.

In individual sports where the performers are in a tournament and lose early on, a different physical programme is needed.

As a coach, you may find it necessary to challenge competitive schedules that have been developed by parents, especially in individual sports. The involvement of the coach in planning the competitive programme is essential, especially when a periodised plan is in place. You will have seen from the principles of LTAD in Section 1, and from the different sports' LTAD charts at the beginning of this section, that the amount and type of competition changes as the young performer matures. Many adults do not yet understand this concept. When working with younger performers, some coaches form a 'developmental team' consisting of the parents, the performer and the coach. This approach can help to solve issues like the volume and timing of competition and ensure

that everyone involved in the performer's development is 'on the same page'. The team approach has the added benefit of helping young performers to feel involved in their own training and competition (see Section 3 on goal setting).

Tapering

In Section 4, we established that the stresses imposed in training lead to adaptation, but also cause fatigue. This fatigue can prevent a performer from achieving peak performance. Many coaches are reluctant to reduce training volumes in the lead-in to competition because they fear that training effects will be reversed. It has been demonstrated, however, that training effects reverse more slowly than was once thought. Training-induced fatigue is lost much more quickly than training effects are. The coach's task is to manage training so that peak performance can occur in a window between the removal of fatigue and the reversal of training effects.

To prepare your performers for important competitions or the major matches of the season, you will need to **taper** their training, so they will peak at the appropriate time. As discussed in Section 4 (page 64), duration and frequency equate to total training volume. In the tapering phase, you will need to manipulate these variables to decrease total training volume in preparation for peak performance.

Tapering also means an increase in simulated training (training which replicates competition) and mental skills practice. Ideally, the training in the taper phase will involve sessions that are at an intensity specific to that of a forthcoming competition. When a taper follows a period of high training volume, it is not uncommon for performers to feel that they are not training hard enough. In the first third of the taper, the body needs time to adjust to the unloading programme.

The duration of the taper phase varies from performer to performer and from sport to sport. The length of time for unloading training volume varies from 5–28 days or more, but, in general terms, a normal taper is 10–21 days. The time required to reach performance readiness will depend on factors such as the:

- length of the preparation phase
- training volume in the previous months
- requirements of the sport
- duration of the peaking
- individual differences, including age and ability.

Some performers will have the ability to peak very quickly on very few days of low-volume training (5–7 days). On the other hand, some will take longer (14–28 days) and it is not uncommon to see superior performances in sport during competitions that follow the major competition phase. This may be due to less psychological stress, greater confidence or greater physiological readiness.

The key to physiological and psychological readiness in competition is the knowledge that all the preparatory work has been done. This will give the performer(s)/team a confidence in their ability to achieve their goals and a determination to succeed. Last-minute preparation does not give performers confidence.

Recovery/transition phase

This will be the one phase during the programme where the performer will take a break from training. The phase is usually short and is concerned with the physical and mental recovery of the performer. Depending on the number of competitive phases in the year, the recovery phase could last for at least three weeks, but this period of time could be split up if there are three or four competitive peaks. With younger performers, the length of the recovery period should increase, especially for those moving through puberty. Preference should be given to general activities (active recovery), where performers engage in other sports or activities of interest that incorporate fun and variety.

If too few demands are placed on the performer during the competitive phase, a transitional phase may be unnecessary and the performer may move straight into the next preparatory phase. However, there should be a brief rest, perhaps of 2–3 days, after each important competitive phase, before moving on.

Often, performers do not feel they have time for this short break, but it is important following a long competitive phase.

Activity 23

1. Using the chart below, mark in the most important competitions in the year for your performer.

Month												
Competition												
Period												
Components												

2 Now, include the training phases you identified in the previous exercise:
- Recovery/transition
- Preparation
  - general phase
  - specific phase
- Competition.

3 In Activity 4 in Section 2, you were asked to list the important Performance Factors in your sport. Insert these factors into the chart, according to the phases when they will be most prominent.

You should now have an idea of how the principles of periodisation apply to your sport. How you periodise your year will depend on many factors, including the:

- *competitive structure of the sport*
- *competitions that you prioritise with your performers*
- *age and stage of development of your performers*
- *number of different components of performance and the priority you place on each.*

Different coaches will divide the training year in different ways for valid reasons. For example, a team-game coach who believes that aerobic fitness is the key to success in that sport would have a much longer general preparatory phase at the expense of the specific preparatory phase. A coach who believes that tactics and teamwork were paramount would do the opposite. The key issue is that the coach is able to ensure that all the Performance Factors are integrated and trained to maximise performance.

Planning mesocycles

Mesocycles are phases of 1–6/7 weeks that allow you to structure training in greater detail. Each mesocycle will *prioritise* different components of training, but will still include others. Therefore, mesocycles differ from each other in tasks, forms of training and training load.

A macrocycle could contain 3–20 mesocycles (the rugby union annual plan on page 94 had 9). The breakdown will depend on how you wish to categorise and group training components. The demands of the sport, the age and stage of development and degree of specialisation of the performer, as well as the length and type of the macrocycle, will all have an influence. In essence, it is a case of allocating specific time to the different training objectives, so the performer can concentrate on developing particular components without interference from other components. There is no right way and experimentation with the phases is often the only way to determine the best breakdown for an individual performer.

Examples of mesocycle construction

In a rugby player's preparation phase, successive mesocycles might increase the intensity of the player's weight training. The aim is to move from the basic strength training of the general preparatory phase to more specific power-based exercises as the competitive season approaches. However, if the player wished to make large aerobic gains, he would concentrate on endurance prior to the weights programme, rather than attempting simultaneous gains. As the competitive season approaches, more energy is devoted to technical and tactical components. So, for this performer, a typical mesocycle structure in the preparatory phase might look like that in Table 4 overleaf.

Table 4: Mesocycle structure in the preparatory phase for a rugby player

Mesocycle name	Number	Content	Duration
General prep 1	1	Introduction	1 week
2	2	Aerobic base work/ intro to strength	3 weeks
3	3	Strength base work	5 weeks
Specific prep 1	4	Power and anaerobic work	3 weeks
2	5	Anaerobic, tactical and technical work	3 weeks

A number of different scenarios can impact on the content of training programmes. Training programmes for beginners will focus on basic techniques and fitness components and will require fewer variations in content and methods than programmes for more advanced performers. With young performers, their age and stage will obviously be a huge factor in determining the content of the mesocycle or even the mesocycle. If the performer is growing rapidly, there could also be changes during the macrocycle itself. Advanced programmes will probably further subdivide the specific preparatory phase and the pre-competitive phase to achieve more specific outcomes. Mature performers will, therefore, have more complex programmes, with a greater number of mesocycles. The number of mesocycles in a season can vary from five for a single-periodised year in a sport with few technical variations to 20 or more for an advanced performer in a sport with many technical variations. The next activity will give you the opportunity to apply these considerations.

Activity 24

Refer to the planner you compiled in Activity 21. This is the basic structure of your programme.

1 Identify the major competitions of the year and mark them with an asterisk on the following planner:

Month												
	1	2	3	4	5	6	7	8	9	10	11	12
Competition Planner												
Major Training Phases												
Performance Components												
Mesocycle Planner												

2 Now, fill in the major training phases that you identified in the previous activity (ie general and specific preparatory, competition and recovery/transition).

3 Try to identify more specifically the stages when you will focus on the important training components – for example, the movement from general to competition-specific techniques and skills. Write these components into the planner in the space provided. This will assist you in your subdivision of the training programme into appropriate mesocycles.

4 Determine the optimal number of mesocycles for your performer/team for the coming season.

Bear in mind the age and stage of development of your performer. Remember that peaking will require very high intensity training and, as we have already mentioned, should not be attempted by novices or young performers more than once or twice in the annual programme. For young performers, the key issue is to know and take account of their level of maturation.

Remember that there is no correct answer. The priority you place on the different performance components will determine how you have allocated your time. If you had difficulty allocating specific sections of time to different training components, remember that you will not ignore a component simply because it is not prioritised for a particular mesocycle. The cycles you have associated with specific components are the times when you will allocate extra time to developing these components.

Look back on your plan and ask yourself how it reflects the priority you place on different performance components. Would you make any amendments as a result of this reflection?

Manipulating volume and intensity

Structuring mesocycles requires manipulation of the volume and intensity of training for different performance components to achieve the required effects in those chosen. The trade-off between volume and intensity in each component will determine whether gains are made in that component or whether the component is maintained at the required level.

A mesocycle will have a general level of intensity and volume, at which most of the training in that cycle will be pitched. This will reflect the intensity of the components that are dominant at that time. In the competitive phase, for example, the majority of the work will be at competition intensity and will focus on competition-specific training.

An example of the volume and intensity of a series of mesocycles is shown in Figure 17.

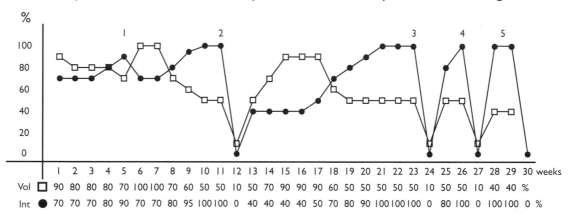

Figure 17: Phases of training within a multiple-phased annual plan for a 30-week competitive season; this plan has one minor peak (1) and four major ones (2/3/4/5)

You should have noticed the changes in volume and intensity at different times in the plan, as well as noting the recovery times.

At this stage, we can begin to include the information you acquired in Sections 2, 3 and 4.

The next activity will take you through the process of planning your mesocycles. If you are unsure about any stage, go back and read that section of the resource again. This activity will draw on your knowledge of your sport (Section 2), planning principles and goal setting (Section 3) and Principles of Training (Section 4).

Activity 25

Mesocycle planning

1 Think about a simple annual plan before starting this activity.

2 Select a mesocycle from your performer's programme that deals with preparation (see Activity 22).

3 Calculate the number of days in the mesocycle.

4 Specify the intensity level of the mesocycle (high, medium, low). This will depend on the distance from competition.

Macrocycle: ....

Mesocycle number: .... Number of days: ....

Intensity level: ....

Mesocycle focus (eg preparation or specific preparation): ....

5 Specify the objectives of the mesocycle. These should conform to SMARTER principles.

Mesocycle objectives:

-
-
-
-
-
-
-

Continued...

6 Identify the Performance Factor components to be developed in this mesocycle and those which should be maintained. Remember to consider all the performance factors.

Performance Factor	Performance Component	Classification	% of time	No of units

7 Identify the number of training units for each component in the mesocycle. *A training unit is one training session in which you aim to develop or maintain that component.* You will decide this based on the Principles of Training, and whether the component is to be maintained or developed in this cycle. In many cases, there will be a trade-off between the different components on the basis of the time available.

8 Identify the length of the microcycles (eg 2–7 days) in the mesocycle. This is a matter for judgement. You will need to consider the work:rest ratio for the general mesocycle programme and for each individual component in the mesocycle. A balanced decision should then be made on the optimal length of the microcycles. The most important physical component is likely to bias the decision, as the work:rest ratio in this will be crucial. Divide the first bar of the following table into the appropriate number of microcycles.

9 Identify the intensity level of each microcycle on a scale of 1–5 (where 5 is 100% intensity). Then decide the percentage volume. Mark in both levels on the chart provided. An example is provided on the next page.

Length of microcycles: .... days

5	
4	
3	
2	
1	

O – Volume   ● – Intensity

Mesocycle plan

Length of microcycles: 7 days

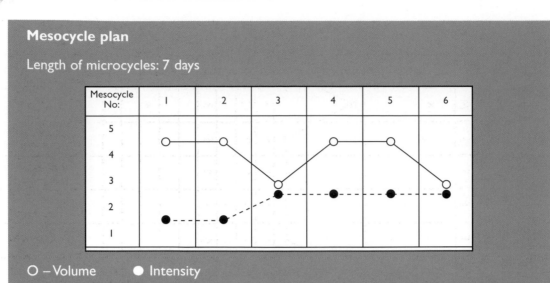

O – Volume   ● Intensity

Figure 18: Volume and intensity levels in a GPP mesocycle

The way you have planned will depend on the demands of your sport. The number of components and the intensity level will vary. Figure 18 is an example of a general preparatory phase mesocycle for a rugby union player. The intensity level is low but building, and the volume is high, but medium-load cycles (3 and 6) are included to allow for adequate recovery.

The following is a typical mesocycle planner for the competitive phase of a volleyball player. It is apparent how the volume and intensity are manipulated according to the principles of overcompensation.

Study this planner. What conclusions/observations would you make? The coach is using a five-day microcycle, with four working days and one rest day. The mesocycle comprises four microcycles.

A blank mesocycle planner is included in Appendix A.

Table 5: Mesocycle planning for a volleyball coach

Macro: Competitive   Meso: 11
Objective: Technical – emphasis on blocking/defence. Conditioning – power and speed development; aerobic maintenance

x – Conditioning
o – Practice

C – Conditioning
P – Practice

Micro		1					2					3					4				
Date (June)		6	7	8	9	10	11	12	13	14	15	16	17	18	19	20	21	22	23	24	25
Weekday		F	S	S	M	T	W	T	F	S	S	M	T	W	T	F	S	S	M	T	W
Volume (x, scale 5–0)		4	3	4	4	0	4	3	4	3	0	4	4	4	3	0	3	3	4	3	0
Intensity (x/o, scale 5–0)		x/o	o	o/x	x/o	o	x/o	o	x/o	o	o	x/o	o	x/o	x	o	x	o	x	o	x
Day		1	2	3	4	5	1	2	3	4	5	1	2	3	4	5	1	2	3	4	5
AM	C	C	C	P	C	-	C	C	C	P	-	C	C	C	-	-	P	P	C	C	-
PM	P	P	P	-	P	-	P	P	P	-	-	P	P	P	P	-	-	-	-	P	P
Practice (1 hr)		3	3	4	3	-	3	3	3	4	-	3	3	3	4	-	4	4	3	3	-
Strength																					
Power		x			x		x		x			x		x					x		
Speed																					
Anaerobic																					
Anaerobic A																					
Aerobic			x					x					x							x	
Activity		Blocking	Blocking	Blocking/Defence	Blocking/Defence			Defence	Blocking	Blocking/Defence			Defence		Blocking		Blocking/Defence	Blocking/Defence		Blocking/Defence	

Planning microcycles

Microcycles may be phases of 2–7 days. There is no set time frame. They should be organised around the objectives of the mesocycle and the principles of adaptation, especially recovery. It is usually convenient to plan microcycles for a phase of one week, as this helps to fit training units and sessions into the general framework of social routine.

Activity 26

Look carefully at the microcycle in Figure 19 on page 115 for a 16-year-old tennis player. What are the key issues that you notice?

© Anne Pankhurst

Female Tennis Player Aged 16

Plan for Microcycle 2

Mesocycle length is 3 weeks — in the preparation phase of the second macrocycle of the annual plan

Training Units:
- warm-up
- coordination
- speed
- strength
- endurance
- flexibility
- tactical
- mental — built in to all work — focus on concentration and routines
- academic — Monday – Friday three hours per day

	Day 1	Day 2	Day 3	Day 4	Day 5	Day 6	Day 7
Intensity	medium intensity	high intensity	low intensity	high intensity	low intensity	2 practice matches	rest day
Units	120 mins	120 mins	90 mins	120 mins	120 mins		
warm-up	15 mins	15 mins	15 mins	15 mins	15 mins		
coordin	10 mins	10 mins	10 mins	10 mins	10 mins		
speed	20 mins	20 mins		20 mins			
tac (combined)	90 mins	90 mins	90 mins	90 mins	90 mins		
tec (combined)							
core	45 mins		45 mins		45 min		
flexibility	15 mins	15 mins	15 mins	15 mins	15 min		
Lunch							
academic	90 mins	90 mins	90 mins	90 mins	90 mins		
academic	90 mins	90 mins	90 mins	90 mins	90 mins		
UNITS	120 mins	120 mins	120 mins	120 mins	120 mins		
tac (combined)	120 mins	120 mins	120 mins	120 mins	120 mins		
tec (combined)							
strength	30 mins	30 mins		30 mins			
endurance			30 mins		30 mins	30 mins	
flexibility	15 min	15 mins	15 mins	15 mins	15 mins	15 mins	15 mins

Figure 19: Microcycle plan for 16-year-old female tennis player

You have probably noticed:

- *the mesocycle covers three weeks of seven days each in the preparation phase*
- *the microcycle is seven days in length and is the second microcycle in the mesocycle*
- *the player is an elite performer*
- *the volume of training for each component is calculated and built into the programme*
- *there is a strong link to LTAD principles because of the age of the player*
- *practice matches are included*
- *rest is built into the week*
- *the programme builds in the fact that the player is still at school, although home schooled. The volume of training would be the same, but the timetable would change if the player attended normal school.*

Having studied this microcycle for a performer in tennis, now try Activity 27 for a microcycle in a pre-competition phase in your own sport.

Activity 27

1 Identify the specific goals of a microcycle in a pre-competitive phase for your sport.

2 Based on the goals you have just set, devise a microcycle from the pre-competition phase for that performer, including all the relevant components of training. Indicate the demand of each training unit on the performer on a scale of high, medium or low.

Day	Goal	Unit	Demand
Monday			
Tuesday			
Wednesday			
Thursday			
Friday			
Saturday			
Sunday			

Now turn over.

The construction of a microcycle is based on the principles of sequencing (the correct ordering and spacing of activities in training sessions). Sessions must be sequenced appropriately if the maximum benefit is to be gained. The interplay of loading, resting, training intensity and training volume must be understood if the process is to be managed effectively.

The following list – adapted from Dick, F.W. (2007) Sports Training Principles[1] – gives a comprehensive list of the many factors which must be considered when sequencing training:

• Demands in individual training units (a specific component) vary from high to slight.

• The performer should not be exposed to very high demands in successive units.

• Each training unit should be in pursuit of a specific objective.

• Programme planning should include variety and have variations in units that are aimed at the same goal.

• Performers require a sense of routine in their programme.

• Intervals between two training units should be long enough to allow the performer to recover and work in the next unit.

• Recovery is accelerated with active recovery or regeneration units.

• When units with different objectives and varying demands follow each other, it may not be necessary to wait for complete recovery.

• Microcycles permit concentration on one particular objective in individual units, allowing some optimal phase of time when the performer can be exposed to the desired stimulus.

• Microcycles reduce monotony in training despite high frequency of training units.

• In terms of physical preparation, demands on speed, power and maximum strength should never follow days of high demand. Speed endurance or strength endurance should never precede techniques, speed, elastic strength or maximal strength either in the same day or on consecutive days.

In team games, a microcycle may require a mini taper to be built in to prepare for competition at the end of the week. Maintenance work on fitness should take place in the early days of the week, so that the training load is lightened prior to competition.

[1] For further information on this, or any other text listed, you should read 6.6 Recap and What Next? at the end of this section.

Examine the following microcycle plan for swimming to see the application of these principles:

Table 6: Microcycle planner for sprint swimmer

Day		Goal	Unit (see scale below)	Demand
Sunday		Rest		
Monday	am	Aerobic	Low aerobic swim Mid aerobic kick	low
	pm	Power Lactic	Lower body weights Threshold swim	high medium
Tuesday		Power	Upper body weights Plyometrics Power swim	high high high
Wednesday		Rest	Sauna Massage	
Thursday	am	Aerobic Power	Low aerobic swim Lower body weights	low high
	pm	Power Aerobic	Plyometrics Mid aerobic swim – odds cruise, even build	high low
Friday	am	Strength Power	Upper body weights Plyometrics	high high
	pm	Power Aerobic	15m power swims Low aerobic drills Mid aerobic pull Starts/turns	high low medium low
Saturday		Aerobic	Mid aerobic kick Swim – lact max swim	medium high

It is useful to rate the intensity of the microcycle on a scale of 1–5, and the volume of training on a similar scale. If the intensity and volume are both high, adequate recovery must be included. A performer will be able to tolerate consecutive microcycles of high intensity only if the volume of training is relatively low.

Planning training sessions

You will now realise that progress in training actually takes place in small steps. While planning must start with a big picture – 10–12 years, quadrennial plans, annual plans and meso and microcycles – each training session is a small step towards achieving the overall goal.

© Alan Edwards

Here is a plan for a single training session in tennis that is taken from the microcycle plan on page 115.

Date: Preparation, week 2 of 3-week mesocycle Microcycle 2 – day 2	Venue:
Time: 7.45	Duration: 2 hours + warm-up and cool-down
Performer: 16-year-old junior tennis player	Training intensity: High
Equipment: Tennis balls, cones, skipping rope	

Goals:
• Development of multi-directional speed post-puberty
• Increased hip and shoulder rotation on serve and return
• Footwork patterns on 3rd and 4th shot preparation

Time	Organisation of Session
7.45–8.10	Warm-up incorporating complex coordination
8.10–8.30	Speed – linear and multi-directional
8.30–10.00	Technical and tactical development: • Serve and return, incorporating routines on serve • 1st-serve placement and preparation for 3rd shot • Block return of 1st serve and preparation for 4th shot • Match timescales used in 2nd 45 minutes
10.00–10.15	Flexibility and cool-down
Evaluation	

Figure 20: Session plan for 16-year-old female tennis player (national junior)

Activity 28

What do you notice in this session plan?

Now turn over.

You may have noticed that:

- the session is the first session of Day 2 of the second microcycle
- there are a number of training units of different Performance Factors in the training session – physical, technical and tactical, with mental skills in terms of improving a routine
- the training units in the session are in a particular order
- the physical skills are trained on court and lead into the technical and tactical work
- the intensity of work is high
- speed training meets the developmental needs of the athlete
- the length of the session is appropriate for the level and age of the player
- if you refer back to the microcycle on page 117, you will notice that this is the first of two training sessions in the day.

Every session should have the same structure and include an evaluation at the conclusion of the session.

Training units

The smallest training phase is the training unit, which is incorporated into a single training session to achieve a training objective. For example, the objective may be to develop concentration skills or sprinting speed.

A performer can work on one or several training units in a session. A basketball player may work through three units in one training session. The first could be work on shooting drills, to develop accuracy, then a second unit could be endurance training (eg 12 x 150m sprints with 30 seconds recovery) and the third unit may be work on ball-receiving skills (moving towards team members to receive the ball early). However, some sessions may be limited by time (eg lunchtime sessions) and perhaps only one unit may be trained.

The session plan for the junior tennis player used in Figure 20 has four training units (or five if training routines is included).

Therefore, a training session may comprise a number of units or only one.

However, training units which require the performer to concentrate on a new component of performance – a new skill or tactic, for example – should not be combined with others. Such training will require the full focus of the performer. In the later stages of honing these skills, additional units may be introduced. Intense physical or mental sessions may not be compatible with complex physical or tactical work, due to the effects of fatigue.

The key issue of any session plan must be the **integration of the units** of the different performance components. These obviously develop from the goals identified by both the performer and the coach.

The *order and priority* in which different components/units will be trained is important. For example, any speed work needs to be undertaken while the performer is fresh but thoroughly warmed up (as it was in the tennis training session); technical work also needs to be trained when the performer is fresh, but when all the muscle groups are warm. Strength training, on the other hand, will make the performer tired and so should be left until the end of the training session. So there is a coaching skill in constructing both the content and the order of a training session.

| Date of session: |
| Time and length of session + microcycle and training phase: |
| Venue: |
| Athlete(s): |
| Main objectives of microcycle: |
| Main objectives of training session: |
| Evaluation: |

Figure 21: Session plan

Recovery from training sessions

We have already discussed the issue of work:rest ratios. Selecting the correct ratio of training to recovery in a single session is very important, in order to facilitate the adaptation process. Different components make different demands on the performer. The performer should not be exposed to successive units of very high demand. The intervals between the same types of training units should be long enough to allow the performer time to recover and perform in the next unit. Remember, recovery is accelerated if it is *active*. When training units with different objectives and varying demands follow each other, complete recovery may not be required (eg a footballer can have a shorter recovery phase after endurance training if the unit following is passing skills). As a rule, more than 24 hours are required to recover from very high training loads, including competitions.

In most team games, a microcycle will revolve around a weekly competitive fixture. Most coaches will allow at least a day's rest prior to competition, and will reduce training loads on the previous day or even two. If this mini-taper occurs in every microcycle, there is little time for intense training in-season. Training time may be further decreased if there are two competitive fixtures in the same week, or when players carry knocks from game to game and so reduce their training capacity. That is why the fitness levels of many team-sport players decline over a season. A coach must plan microcycles very carefully to minimise this effect.

6.4 Maximising Training Time

All coaches would like unlimited access to their performers. In the real world, however, very few have such a luxury. Training time is precious and there is rarely enough of it, because each performer has other commitments to meet outside sport. As a coach, you have a responsibility to your performers to ensure the time they commit to training is maximised (used as efficiently as possible). Practice should be purposeful and meaningful – remember, quantity is not the same as quality.

Each training cycle has objectives that relate to specific components of the Performance Factors. The training time in the cycle is devoted to the pursuit of these objectives. However, the different components need not be viewed in isolation. For example, a football player must concentrate on many components of performance (endurance, concentration, anxiety control, passing and so on) during each cycle. If each training session concentrated solely on one, players would probably never achieve their goals. Training sessions will nearly always contain more than one training component; often, they will combine several.

It is perfectly possible and also necessary, as we have already noted, to integrate different components, and so maximise training time. The footballer's endurance training unit can be combined with a technical or mental unit, for example. Indeed, it is only in the early stages of training a specific component that you will want to train the component in isolation from other components. A football team may have developed concentration skills in the off-season by following very specific mental-skills training programmes. As pre-season work commences, the coach would gradually apply these concentration skills to all training sessions, perhaps beginning with some technical drills and then progressing into practices that simulate competition. The coach could train passing skills to work on players' concentration by adding distractions, such as other players or background noises. After all, such skills will need to operate simultaneously in competition.

Activity 30

1 Select a component from a Performance Factor from your performer's programme, and briefly outline one training session for that component, from any stage in the season.

2 Now, consider other components that could be integrated into that training time, without affecting the training of the original component.

Now turn over.

127

You may have decided to combine mental skills with physical or technical, or technical with physical. There are few components that it is difficult to combine.

However, it is important, when attempting to develop components simultaneously, not to create confusion in your performers by asking them to focus on too many goals at once. The following pointers may be useful in preventing a dilution of focus:

• Introduce one aspect of the activity at a time.

• Be very specific in your instructions.

• Seek regular feedback from your performers on their perception of the activity.

Examine the following plans for a training session for a swimmer and a football team. These sessions demonstrate how combinations of activities within the same unit can achieve several goals in limited training phases.

Date:	23/09	Venue:	25m pool
Main Objectives of Microcycle:		**Main Objectives of Session:**	
maintain basic endurance levels fine-tune turning/stroke technique improve basic speed by 5%		maintenance endurance session stroke technique – holding long basic speed session	
Activity	**Unit 1 – 1 hour**	**Activity**	**Unit 2 – $^1/_2$ hour**
W/U: 12 x 75 on 1.15 3 F/C, 3 o/choice, 6 IM order kick 2 x 200 back with 30s rest (1.3km/22) End: 8 x 400 F/C on 5.00 descend for time 1–4–8 (4.5km/57) (Mentally focus on streamlining from turns)		speed/stroke 28 x 25 on 60 No1 stroke technique: max. effort rest 2 minutes at 15 (5.2km/87) (Sprinting but holding stroke long and counting strokes per length)	
Reminders	**Injuries/Other Comments**		**Evaluation**
All swimmers to fill in logbooks this week. Lactate tests next session.	PS low on iron – see dietitian. Video breaststrokers to check injury problems.		Swimmers are adapting well to early prep. work. Should have no difficulties entering next phase.

Figure 22: Sample session plan for a swimmer

The following training session is typical of that of a preparation/pre-season phase for a football team:

Date:	20/10		Venue:	All-weather surface
Main Objectives of Microcycle:			Main Objectives of Session:	
maintain aspects of fitness: speed, endurance, flexibility and agility principles of play – possession			endurance maintenance individual positional play to keep possession in attacking third develop concentration on positional play	
Activity	**Unit 1 – 60 mins**			
1 Warm-up	jogging, stretching, ball touching exercises (10 mins)			
2 Speed	5 x 50 metres striding, 5 x 50 metres extended stride (10 mins)			
3 Recovery	ball work in small groups – maintaining possession (5 mins)			
4 Endurance	continuous jogging in positional groups (20 mins)			
5 Recovery	ball work as above (5 mins)			
6 Education	fluid replacement (10 mins)			
	Unit 2 – 60 mins			
1 Speed	2 x 300 metres (6 x 50 metres) – build up to 9/10 of full speed (10 mins)			
2 Recovery	team play 11v11– maintaining possession attacking 3rd (5 mins)			
3 Tech/Tactics	positional play, set pieces, attacking 3rd (25 mins)			
4 Endurance	continuous jog increasing to striding (15 mins)			
5 Cool-down	stretching and slow jog (5 mins)			
Reminders	**Injuries/Other Comments**		**Evaluation**	
Bring running shoes for next training session – long run off road.	TR, AL to see physio next session.		New members of team settling in well. Set pieces and positional play need more work.	

Figure 23: Sample session plan for a football team

The following activity will help you to apply the above information to your own sport.

Activity 31

1 Refer to Activity 27 and select one training session from the microcycle you planned.

2 In the following planner, decide on the programme of activities for this session that will maximise the time available and accommodate the different objectives of the session.

Date: _____ Venue: _____ Attendance: _____

Main objectives of microcycle:

-
-
-

Main objectives of session:

-
-
-

Activity Outline	

Reminders	Injuries/Other Comments	Evaluation

6.5 Completing the Annual Plan

You now have all the information you need to complete your annual plan for a performer in your sport. Even if you are working to a longer schedule (of two or four years), it is important to plan your yearly programme in this way. You will need all the information you have generated in the previous sections of the resource to complete the plan.

Before you draw up your plan, go back to the two annual plans at the beginning of Section 6.3 that show an annual training and competition plan for a club rugby union team, which plays in a league and two cup competitions, and for a young tennis player trying to become a tour player. In the rugby union plan, the coach has targeted the league and national cup competitions. The team expects to finish in the top two in the league. The coach has targeted league games 6 and 14 (against their closest rivals) for mini-tapers. The annual plan for the tennis player shows you a programme for an individual in a multi-periodised sport, who is aiming to achieve a world ranking within the top 500 in the next 12 months.

There is a blank plan in Appendix A that will help you in the next activity and can also be used in the future. Activity 32 will take you through the process and explain the planner.

Activity 32

The annual plan

Using the blank annual plan, try to complete the following tasks:

1 Fill in the months and weeks of all competitive fixtures and their locations.

2 Rate each competitive fixture on a scale of 1–5 (five being the most important).

3 On the basis of the fixture rating, insert an asterisk at the weeks where a peak is to be achieved.

4 Identify the preparation, competition and transition periods.

5. Identify the macrocycle(s).

6. Break down the macrocycle(s) into mesocycles.

7 Fill in the main goals of each mesocycle.

Table 7: Blank annual plan

Month	January				February				March				April				May				June				July				August				September				October				November				December			
Week	1	2	3	4	5	6	7	8	9	10	11	12	13	14	15	16	17	18	19	20	21	22	23	24	25	26	27	28	29	30	31	32	33	34	35	36	37	38	39	40	41	42	43	44	45	46	47	48	49	50	51	52
Comp phase + Training phase macro																																																				
Training phase meso																																																				
Intensity 1-5																																																				
Volume 1-5																																																				
Peaking																																																				
Testing																																																				
Goals																																																				
Physical																																																				
Technical																																																				
Tactical																																																				
Mental																																																				

If you found these tasks somewhat difficult, you might like to review the rugby union and tennis examples and try the activity again. If this is the first time you have written an annual plan, take each step slowly and always work from the bigger picture of the months of the year down to the detail of the mesocycles. Once your plan is in place, you will find it relatively easy to plan microcycles and single sessions.

6.6 Recap and What Next?

Working through the different levels of planning should help you to understand:
- the relationship between these different levels and the importance of considering each one of them
- the necessity of understanding the 'big picture' in planning
- how each piece of the plan fits to the one below and the one above.

To improve performance:
- training units are part of organised and sequenced training sessions
- training sessions make up each microcycle
- microcycles link to form mesocycles which, in turn, are parts of macrocycles
- each cycle is structured to meet specific objectives
- each macrocycle forms part of the annual plan
- the annual plan fits into a quadrennial plan
- overseeing all of these is the long-term development of the performer – the 10–12-year plan
- each plan is, therefore, part of the whole in developing talent and helping every performer reach their goals
- a balance between training and recovery must be maintained continuously throughout a performer's life
- the effects of training will not be seen immediately and the emphasis should always be placed on *long-term* improvement.

For further information on some of the topics covered in this section, the following resources and articles may prove useful:

Balyi, I. (2002) 'Long-term Athlete Development: the system and solution', *FHS*, 14: 6–9.

Cabral, P. and Crisfield, P. (2005) *Motivation and Mental Toughness*. 2nd edition. Leeds: Coachwise Business Solutions/The National Coaching Foundation.
ISBN: 978-902523-24-5.

Dick, F.W. (2007) *Sports Training Principles*. 5th edition. London, A & C Black.
SBN: 978-0713682-78-6.

Pankhurst, A. and The British Canoe Union (2006) *Preparing for a Life in Sport: A guide to good practice for all people involved in paddlesport* (LTPD leaflet). Leeds: Coachwise Business Solutions/The National Coaching Foundation.

Pankhurst, A. and The British Judo Association (2006) *Preparing for a Life in Sport: A guide to good practice for all people involved in judo* (LTPD leaflet). Leeds: Coachwise Business Solutions/The National Coaching Foundation.

Stafford, I. and Balyi, I. (2005) *Coaching for Long-term Athlete Development*. Leeds: Coachwise Business Solutions/The National Coaching Foundation. ISBN: 978-1-902523-70-9.

sports coach UK (2002) *Physiology and Performance*. 3rd edition. Leeds: Coachwise Business Solutions/The National Coaching Foundation. ISBN: 978-947850-24-4.

All these resources are available from Coachwise 1st4sport (tel 0113-201 5555 or visit www.1st4sport.com).

Further reading

Bompa, T. (2000) *Total Training for Young Champions*. Champaign, Illinois: Human Kinetics. ISBN: 978-0-736002-12-7.

Cross, N. and Lyle, J. (1999) *The Coaching Process: principles and practice for sport*. Oxford: Butterworth-Heinemann. ISBN: 978-0-750641-31-9.

Kidman, L. and Hanrahan, S. (1997) *The Coaching Process*. Wellington: Dunmore Press. ISBN: 978-0-864694-61-4.

Malina R.M., Bouchard, C. and Bar-Or, O. (2004) *Growth, Maturation and Physical Activity Second Edition*. Champaign, Illinois: Human Kinetics. ISBN: 978-0-88011882-8.

Section 7

Reviewing and Monitoring Progress

7.0 What this Section is About

In Section 6, we referred to the need to review and monitor your plans on a regular basis. Reviewing should be part of the planning process – ie time should be built in when you and the performer/team assess whether the plan is feasible, or should be adapted.

Monitoring the progress of your performer/team in the context of the plan is important, because you need to know how close you are to where you want to be at any moment in time.

Monitoring is a simple concept and should be a simple process. Coaches are sometimes blinded by science and often put their performers through comprehensive testing sessions without determining what is strictly necessary. When deciding on how to monitor the progress of your performers, you should use three steps:

• What do you need to know?

• How will you find it out (what measures it)?

• How will you record it and communicate it to your performers?

In Section 2, you selected various tests and performance-assessment methods which provided you with a snapshot profile of your performers. As performers move gradually towards their goals, you will need to know how this snapshot is changing. You will require information on the areas that are improving and any that are not. You will want to monitor the rate of improvement, so you can evaluate the programme of training you have planned and the interventions you have made.

In order to make these judgments, you need some **performance indicators**. Performance indicators are easily interpreted measurements which allow you to make judgements on your performers' progress towards their goals. Monitoring these indicators enables you to use evidence to adjust the training programme, as necessary.

By the end of this section, you should be able to:

- state the performance indicators you will use to monitor your performers
- devise appropriate ways to record your performers' progress
- devise ways to encourage your performers to engage in self-monitoring and record keeping.

7.1 Performance Indicators

This section examines **why** you might monitor your performers, **how** to monitor them (which indicators to use) and **when** you might monitor these performance indicators.

© Alan Edwards

Why monitor progress?

You have already identified several reasons for assessing performers. Coaches test and monitor their performers in order to:

- identify strengths and weaknesses of performers, to identify priorities
- provide baseline data for individual training programmes
- isolate and assess individual components that cannot be measured in the competitive situation
- prescribe the optimal training programme (eg intensity, volume)
- obtain feedback to evaluate the existing training programme
- assess the performer's progress – feedback for the performer/coach
- motivate the performer to train
- check the performer has been training correctly (eg putting in the required effort)
- evaluate progress, in terms of growth and development
- establish homogeneous groupings for training
- assess recovery from injury/layoff.

Your motives for carrying out various tests and assessments will depend on your sport, the situation and your performers. The next activity requires you to identify some of these reasons.

Activity 33

Reread the preceding list and make a list of the reasons why you use assessments in your sport.

Now turn over.

You have probably identified many of the reasons listed in the previous section, and some others. Coaches use testing for different reasons – some are very anxious that they have some objective measures with which to evaluate their training programmes; some use them as motivational tools.

Coaches who have less contact with their performers may use testing more as a monitoring tool than coaches who meet their performers every day. The latter are more likely to be able to make accurate subjective judgements on their performers' current state. Coaches who have infrequent contact with their performers are more likely to use tests to check performers' adherence to training and the efficacy of the training programmes.

How to monitor progress

Your first step is to decide exactly what you need to monitor in order to assess your performers' progress. If your performer is a middle-distance runner, you may decide it is important for you to have a regular measure of aerobic endurance. It may be that your performer's attitude to training is important to you, so you may wish to monitor several components.

You must then decide on the performance indicators you will use in this process. At this stage, you may wish to refer back to Activity 6 on page 31. You may use some of the performance assessments identified on this list as performance indicators. You could test several components at the same time. For example, a 12-minute run might provide you with an adequate measure of your performer's aerobic endurance and you could use a self-rating scale to measure attitude at the same time. You may wish to use other measures, such as performers' pulse rates or sleep patterns, as indicators for other components. You may wish to monitor some components at frequent intervals, while it may be more appropriate to measure others infrequently. Whatever you decide, your programme of assessments should provide you with sufficient information about your performers' progress towards their goals.

Activity 34

1 Decide which areas you need to monitor to assess your performers' progress. List them in the following table.

2 Now, list the performance indicator you wish to use in each area.

	Area	Indicator		Area	Indicator
1			11		
2			12		
3			13		
4			14		
5			15		
6			16		
7			17		
8			18		
9			19		
10			20		

Make sure you are not overambitious in your intentions. Only seek information you need.

When to monitor performance indicators

Many of these performance indicators will require a programme of testing. The decision on when to test is very much a function of the performance indicators you are using, and the reasons why you are testing. If you are considering an annual plan, bear in mind your periodisation of the annual plan when deciding on when to test. You have divided your training year into phases where different components are prioritised. It may be useful to test some components at regular intervals during a training period that has prioritised those components. It is rarely useful to test components in a maintenance phase.

Testing too frequently will probably fail to show measurable improvements in athletic performance, whereas too long a spell between tests will limit opportunities to evaluate the training programme and to modify it if it is not proving effective. Usually, performance improvements will take at least 6–8 weeks to materialise, so testing should be structured with this in mind. Most elite performers undergo 2–6 tests for a component each year.

Minor competitions can be interpreted as assessments, especially with young performers. For example, a county competition could be used by young performers to test their current state of training.

Activity 35

1 Turn to Activity 24 on page 107 and identify when you would test the physical, mental, tactical and technical performance components. If you want to test all the performance components within the same microcycle, then simply fill in one square. If, however, you would like to test individual components at varying periods during the season, use a different colour or code to show each component.

2 Would you prefer to administer tests or assessments at:
- specified times during the year
- regular intervals
- one-off testing sessions?

Explain your reasons.

3 Did you involve your performer in deciding on the testing routine?

7.2 Recording the Data

You have identified indicators you will use to monitor your performer's progress. This will produce a lot of data that must be analysed and recorded. You will also want to record other information, such as attendance records and competition results. Coaches can and do record countless items about their performers and their programmes.

Recording information is time-consuming, however. You must decide what you need and want to record within your programme. Otherwise, you run the risk of holding lots of useless records, or of failing to record some important data because it was not specific to the task in hand at the time. Most swimming coaches will record swimmers' times in competitive meets, for example, and will usually discuss the swimmers' mental state with them after the event. Some coaches might note some comments on this discussion. This information is relevant only if it is correlated with the records on the results.

© www.actionplus.co.uk

Activity 36

Make a list of the things that, in an ideal world, you would like to record in your programme.

Now turn over.

You will probably have listed many of the following and perhaps some others:

- *the annual periodisation plan (including periods, cycles and phases)*
- *monthly planning sheets*
- *weekly planning sheets*
- *session planners*
- *attendance records*
- *competition planners*
- *names, addresses, email addresses and telephone numbers of performers, coaches, facility staff officials, parents, schools*
- *progress sheets for all aspects of performance – technical, tactical, physical and mental*
- *growth and development records, especially height and weight for young performers reaching maturation*
- *competition result sheets*
- *goal-setting contract sheets*
- *testing preparation sheets and testing results (data)*
  - *fitness, mental skills, tactical and technical skills*
  - *biomechanical assessments*
  - *nutritional assessments*
  - *medical screening*
- *injury report sheets.*

Add any of these to your list if you feel they would be useful. Again, what you record will depend entirely on your situation, sport and performers. For example, in a team sport, it is difficult to record everything on every player – you would not have any time left in which to coach. You must develop a system that works best for you – keep it simple but effective. Remember, the log is to help you, not constrain or confuse you by holding unnecessary information.

You probably work with a number of performers as individuals or as part of a squad. This makes it difficult to keep regular and accurate records of each one of them, yet such information is vital if progress is to be monitored successfully and objectively. However, it is important that you do not create too much work for yourself – use your performers or other members of your coaching team to assist in the recording of information.

The following pages contain various sample sheets which you may find useful for logging information from your programme. More sheets are available in Appendix A for photocopying. Amend any that would be useful with some adaptation.

Performer Personal Details

Name	Address	email address	Telephone (Home/Work)	Date of birth	Education (Work Education/ Unemployed)
John Smith	39 Wood Road Leeds LS1 4AP		(H) 0113-994 9994	12/10/80	Student, Business Studies, Leeds Met, Year Three. Lives at home

Nutrition Assessment Sheet

Date:		Cycle:		Period:	

Date:
Type of day (eg weekday, holiday)
Level of training load (eg rest day, high intensity)

Time	Training	Detailed Description of Food/Fluid Consumed
0600	8k run – h/r 165 28min	Orange juice, wholemeal bread and butter – 2 slices Cereal: All-Bran 80g 2 bananas, an apple
0800		

Personal Best Record Sheet

Name	Date	Competition	Event	Result	Position
eg Jill Smith	3.2.97	Grand Prix Swim Meet (Long Course – Leeds)	100m B/fly	1:02.35	3rd Junior
eg Ian Brown Centre	5.7.97	Durham Colts RFU County Plate	2nd Round – Framwell	Scored 2 Tries	Won 18–12

Figure 24: Sample monitoring tools (a blank nutrition assessment sheet is in Appendix B and blank performer record sheets are available to photocopy in Appendix C)

Displaying progress

Coaches use a diary to log things such as individual session plans or competitive goals. Items such as attendance sheets and testing data are usually stored on a computer or in a file. All these pieces of information can provide records of progress. For motivational purposes, coaches will usually want to share this information with their performers. Noticeboards are useful for this purpose.

Many coaches use graphs to display data they want to share with their squads. This gives performers and the coach a visual display of progress and can be useful in portraying the overall picture. For example, performance times in training for a specific distance could be graphed over a mesocycle or even a season. Figure 25 shows how a football coach might illustrate a player's 30-metre sprint speed, tested weekly over a season. The advantage of a graphical display is that trends in the data can be recognised more easily, so the performer does not become too focused on the last result. In week 17 of the graph in Figure 25, the result was worse than in the previous week. However, the graph reinforces the downward trend, and the poor result for that week should not worry the performer unduly.

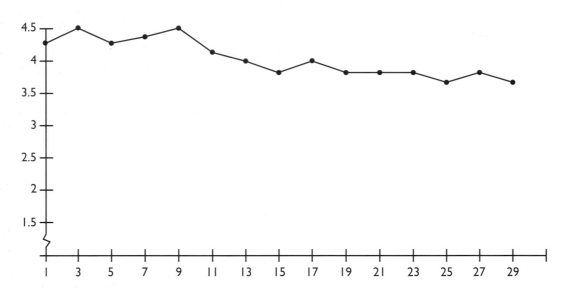

Figure 25: Progress of 30-metre sprinting speed over a season for a footballer

Once you have developed your own organisational and management skills, the people around you (eg assistant coaches, performers) will also become more effective at planning and recording information. Throughout this resource, you have been encouraged to include your performers in many planning activities (such as performance profiling and goal setting) and, again, it is important that you encourage them to record their own information about their training programmes.

7.3 Performers' Logbooks

Performers in individual sports will often keep a diary or logbook. This practice is not so evident in team games, although some coaches do encourage performers to record information about their training and performances. If you discuss your methods of assessment, planning and recording with your performers, it may be possible to combine your requirements with some entries they make in their personal logbook or training diary. This saves you time and will prevent replication. Be sure, though, that your performers are honest and do not simply record what they think the coach wants to read.

Your performers can monitor aspects of training, competition and lifestyle such as their own:

- body weight

- resting heart rate

- sleep patterns

- attitude to training

- weekly commitments (eg checking information generated in the lifestyle progress chart)

- pre-competition strategy sheets

- competition evaluation sheets (eg structured debriefing)

- notes on opponents.

Activity 37

1 If your performers already keep logs, make a list of the things they record and how often (eg every coaching session, once a week, after competition).

Information Recorded	How Often

2 Whether or not they do, make a list of the things you feel would be useful for them to record (eg training goals, competition goals, performance progress, post-competition evaluation) and how frequently (eg every session, competition or weekly).

Information Recorded	How Often

Now turn over.

It may be useful to ask yourself some questions:

- *Are your suggestions realistic?*
- *Might it become a chore?*
- *Should they always carry their logbook with them?*
- *How frequently do you/should you go through their logbook with them?*

You need to decide what would be helpful (and motivating) for your performers. It will also prove invaluable if you combine some recording of your own with that of your performer – in other words, your performer is entrusted to record his/her own progress.

Sample self-monitoring sheets

On the following pages, you will find both a completed self-monitoring sheet and a sample self-monitoring sheet. You may find it a useful framework for your performers' record keeping or you may wish to customise it in some way. If you work with junior performers, you may decide to omit some of the list below to make the exercise more appropriate to their age and stage of development.

When using the sheet, your performers should:

- plot their resting heart rate, body weight and sleep pattern first thing each morning
- use a different symbol or different coloured pen/pencil for each variable
- record their menstrual cycle (for female performers)
- plot from left to right, but use the appropriate scale for each variable (ie resting heart rate and sleep, read from the left-hand axis)
- ensure the days of the month are indicated and synchronised with both graphs
- plot their attitude to training at the end of each day
- keep the monitoring sheet handy (eg beside the bed)
- record all four variables consistently over a 3–4-month period to identify normal stress-response ranges.

Table 8: Sample self-monitoring sheet (adapted from Australian Coaching Council: Recovery Weekly Planner Pack by Angela Calder)[1]

Name: John Smith

× Resting Heart Rate (bpm)

Month: August

Monthly Starting Point (0) 52 HR 75 BW

O Body Weight (kg)

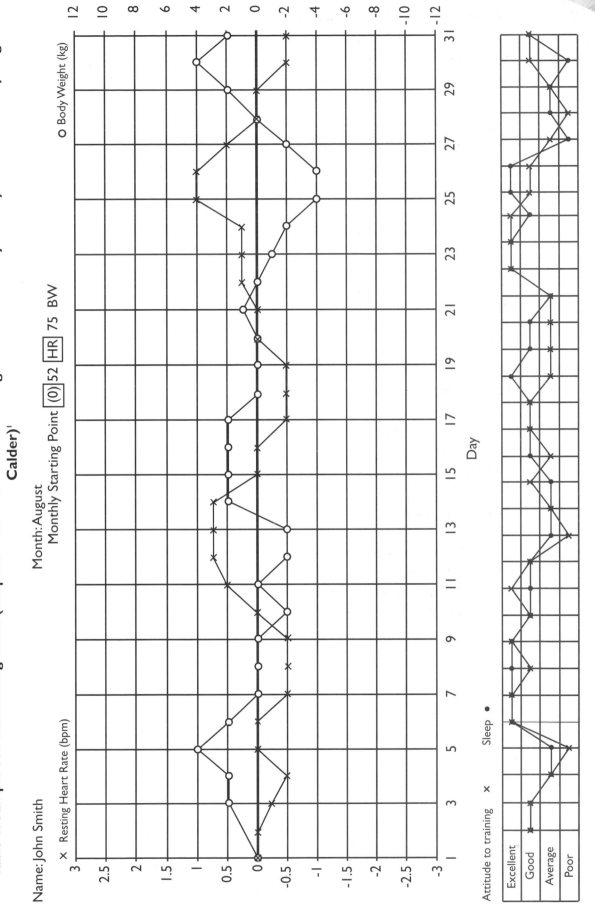

Attitude to training ×   Sleep ●

[1] Calder, A. (1994) *Recovery Programmes.* Home study pack for the Australian Coaching Council's Graduate Diploma of Sports Coaching.

Table 9: Blank self-monitoring sheet

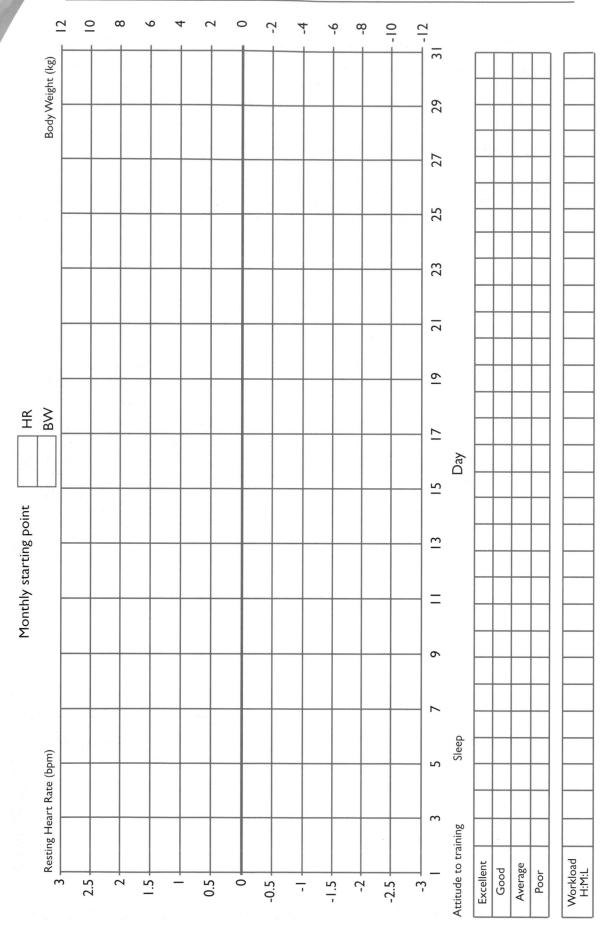

Instructions and important points for using self-monitoring sheets

The self-monitoring sheet is a useful tool in identifying the signs of overtraining and overuse problems and in the early detection of illness. The monitoring process will encourage your performers to take responsibility and help to *tune them in to their bodies and minds*. It is also important to make sure it is age-appropriate.

Although the responsibility for monitoring certain aspects of performance (eg recovery, training, environment) may be placed on the performer, it is very important that you periodically check your performers' logbooks. Similarly, it is important that you emphasise the need for your performers to inform you of any irregularities in their personal records (eg constant tiredness, weight loss, high resting heart rates) as quickly as possible.

Self-assessment forms

Performers can be encouraged to assess their own performance in competition. This process will help them to analyse their performance, to be self-critical and to relate their performance to their personal goals.

Encouraging performers to *look in the mirror* is an effective way of generating commitment to improvement. Many coaches use this process informally. If you wish to formalise the process, review the following example used by a football coach.

Activity 38

Example of a post-match assessment sheet for a football defender.

1 Write down your goal(s) or specific task(s) for the match (eg marking a specific opponent).

2 Did you achieve your goal(s)? Yes/No
  If you elected to change your goal(s) prior to the start, explain why.

3 How do you feel about your performance?

Very satisfied				Very disappointed
5	4	3	2	I

4 Describe the conditions (eg pitch condition, weather, re-organisation due to injury or sending-off).

How well did you cope with the conditions?

Very satisfied				Very disappointed
5	4	3	2	I

5 How well did you stick to your pre-match plans:

• prior to arrival at the ground?

Exactly				Not at all
5	4	3	2	I

If less than 4, explain why:

• at the ground?

Exactly				Not at all
5	4	3	2	I

If less than 4, explain why:

6 How well did you carry out your warm-up?

Very well   Very badly

5   4   3   2   1

Explain why:

7 How well did you concentrate:

• during the warm-up?

Very well   Very badly

5   4   3   2   1

• during the early stages of the match?

Very well   Very badly

5   4   3   2   1

• during the middle phase of the match?

Very well   Very badly

5   4   3   2   1

• towards the end of the match?

Very well   Very badly

5   4   3   2   1

8 For what percentage of the time did you keep control of your emotions?

100%   80%   60%   40%   20%   10%

Expand if necessary:

9 Write down any other positive thoughts about the competition.

10 Write down any other negative thoughts about the competition.

11 How much did you enjoy the competition?

This is a comprehensive post-event assessment sheet. It may be that the information you require from your performers can be collected in a more concise form. Again, do not collect information for the sake of it. Review your requirements and construct a mechanism for collating the necessary information.

When considering pre- or post-event assessments, remember that a performer will often find it easier to be honest when writing on a form than when talking face-to-face. A form also allows time to think, without the pressure of having to generate an immediate response. For these reasons, it can be better than an interview. The issue of performers being honest is important and is reflected in the coach/performer relationship being sound enough to sustain open dialogue.

7.4 Recap and What Next?

This section focused on:

- monitoring the progress of your performers and programmes

- examining testing procedures and recording strategies – it is important that you become familiar with the guidelines for testing and develop your own procedures which are both systematic and effective

- recording information for which there is no right or wrong answer – it is important to log and record training information in order to monitor progress, but at a level that suits you, your performers and your sport.

The following resources will complement the information given in this section and are available from Coachwise 1st4sport (tel 0113-201 5555 or visit www.1st4sport.com):

Brewer, C. (2005) *Strength and Conditioning for Games Players*. Leeds: Coachwise Business Solutions/The National Coaching Foundation. ISBN: 978-1902523-85-9.

The National Coaching Foundation (2005) *Multistage Fitness Test*. Leeds: Coachwise Business Solutions/The National Coaching Foundation.

To continue to update and develop your coaching knowledge and skills, you are advised to take note of the workshops and resources recommended throughout the book. These will help to extend your knowledge further on specific topics and improve your coaching. Recommended sports coach UK workshops and resources (complimentary with the corresponding workshop) include:

sports coach UK Workshop	Resource
A Guide to Mentoring Sports Coaches	A Guide to Mentoring Sports Coaches
Analysing your Coaching	Analysing your Coaching
Coaching and the Law	–
Coaching Children and Young People	Coaching Young Performers
Coaching Disabled Performers	Coaching Disabled Performers
Coaching Methods and Communication	The Successful Coach
Equity in Your Coaching	Equity in Your Coaching
Field-based Fitness Testing	A Guide to Field-based Fitness Testing
Fitness and Training	Physiology and Performance
Fuelling Performers	Fuelling Performers
Imagery Training	Imagery Training
Improving Practices and Skill	Improving Practices and Skill
Motivation and Mental Toughness	Motivation and Mental Toughness
Performance Profiling	Performance Profiling

sports coach UK Workshop	Resource
The Responsible Sports Coach	–
Safeguarding and Protecting Children	Safeguarding and Protecting Children
Understanding Eating Disorders	–

All sports coach UK resources are available from:

Coachwise 1st4sport
Chelsea Close
Off Amberley Road
Armley
Leeds LS12 4HP
Tel: 0113-201 5555
Fax: 0113-231 9606
Email: enquiries@1st4sport.com
Website: www.1st4sport.com

sports coach UK also produces a technical journal – *coaching edge* (formerly *FHS*).
Details of this service are available from:

sports coach UK
114 Cardigan Road
Headingley
Leeds LS6 3BJ
Tel: 0113-274 4802
Fax: 0113-275 5019
Email: coaching@sportscoachuk.org
Website: www.sportscoachuk.org

For general information about sports coach UK workshops, or for details of workshops
running in your area, contact:

sports coach UK Business Support Centre
Sport Development Centre
Loughborough University
Loughborough LE11 3TU
Tel: 01509-226 130
Fax: 01509-226 134
Email: bsc@sportscoachuk.org

Appendix A

Planning Tools

Blank LTAD Plan

	FUNdamentals years of age	Learning to Train years of age	Training to Train years of age	Training to Compete years of age	Training to Win years of age	Retainment Own choice
Important	*Important to develop:* • basic movement skills	*Important for:* • building technique • movement skills	*Important for:* • fitness preparation and development • development of sport-specific movement Be aware of growth-spurt issues.	*Important for:* • developing performance • optimising fitness preparation	*Important for:* • refining performance • physical development	*Important for:*
Volume/intensity of training	High volume, low intensity.	According to growth. Could be high volume, increasing intensity.	According to growth. Lower volume, increasing intensity.	High volume, increasing intensity.	High volume, high intensity.	High volume, high intensity.
Number of sessions and length	30–60-minute sessions.	30–90-minute sessions.	120-minute sessions.			
Type of competition / Amount of competition	Unlimited, informal and fun.					
Venues in the training environment						
Coaches – experience and qualifications						

156

Blank Annual Plan

Month	January			February					March				April					May			June					July				August				September			October				November				December			
Week	1	2	3	4	5	6	7	8	9	10	11	12	13	14	15	16	17	18	19	20	21	22	23	24	25	26	27	28	29	30	31	32	33	34	35	36	37	38	39	40	41	42	43	44	45	46	47	48	49	50	51	52
Comp phase + Training phase macro																																																				
Training phase meso																																																				
Intensity 1-5																																																				
Volume 1-5																																																				
Peaking																																																				
Testing																																																				
Goals																																																				
Physical																																																				
Technical																																																				
Tactical																																																				
Mental																																																				

Blank Mesocycle Plan

Macrocycle:
Objective:

Mesocycle:

Date	Weekday	Volume	Intensity	Day	AM	PM								Activity
		5 4 3 2 1 0	5 4 3 2 1 0											

Blank Microcycle Plan

Plan for microcycle   (number)

Performer
age
Mesocycle length and number

Training Units
warm-up
speed
strength
endurance
flexibility
technical
tactical
mental
other

Day 1	Day 2	Day 3	Day 4	Day 5	Day 6	Day 7
intensity	intensity	intensity	intensity	intensity	intensity	intensity
Training unit mins	Training unit mins	Training unit mins	Training unit mins	Training unit mins	Training unit mins	Training unit mins

Blank Session Plan

Date of session:
Time and length of session + microcycle and training phase:
Venue:
Athlete(s):
Main objectives of microcycle:
Main objectives of training session:
Evaluation:

Appendix B

Assessment Tools

Self-monitoring Tool

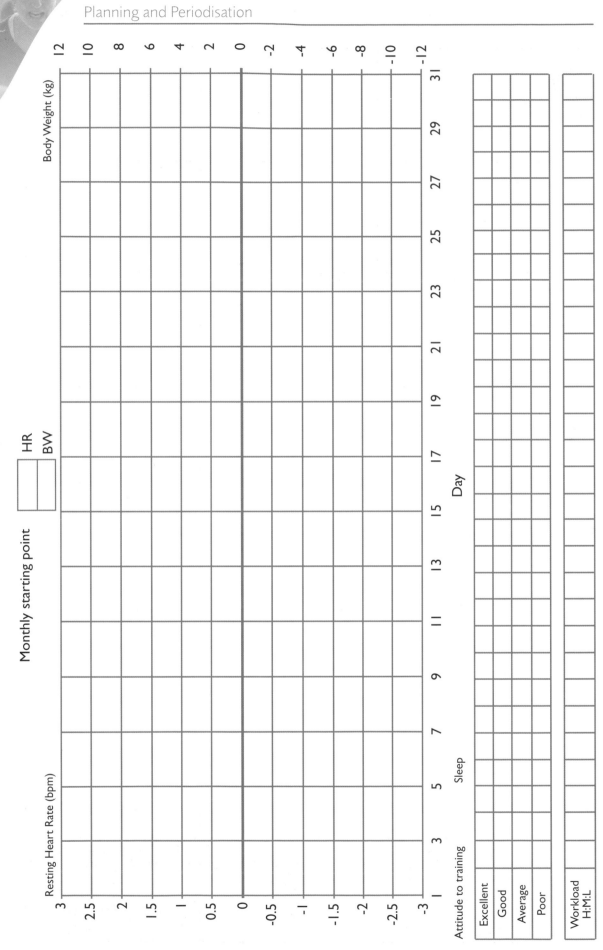

Monthly starting point

	HR
	BW

Resting Heart Rate (bpm)

Body Weight (kg)

Day

Sleep

Attitude to training

| Excellent |
| Good |
| Average |
| Poor |

| Workload H:M:L |

Lifestyle Audit

	Mon	Tues	Wed	Thurs	Fri	Sat	Sun
Morning							
Afternoon							
Evening							

Lifestyle Progress Chart

	Family	Qualifications Examinations	Career/progress Ambition	Sporting Goals	Training Structure	Finances
Yr 1						
Yr 2						
Yr 3						
Yr 4						

Nutrition Assessment Sheet

Date:		Cycle:		Period:	

Date:	
Type of day: (eg weekday, holiday)	
Level of training load: (eg rest day, high intensity)	

Time	Training	Detailed Description of Food/Fluid Consumed

Opposition Analysis (Performer)

Date:		Time:	
Opposition:		Venue:	

Player	Strengths	Weaknesses

Other Factors

Opposition Analysis (Team)

Date:		Time:	
Opposition:		Venue:	

Team Strengths	Team Weaknesses

Other Factors

© Alan Edwards

Appendix C

Performer Record Sheets

Performer Details

Name:		Home phone:	
Address:			
Work/school:		Phone:	
Next-of-kin:		Phone:	
Date of birth:			

Club:		Position/Event:	
History:			

Personal Best Performances/Representative Honours

Date	Venue	Details	Comment

Medical Details

Date	Condition	Medication	Comment

Performer Assessment Record

Performer name:	

Physical							
Test	Dates						

Technical							
Test	Dates						

Mental							
Test	Dates						

Injury Report

Date:		Event:	
Name of injured person:			
Details of injury:			
Where it happened:			
What happened:			
Time:			
Witness(es):			
Action taken:			
Treatment/action /referral:			
(if appropriate) Name of medical personnel involved:			
Hospital/centre attended:			
Guardian informed:			
Post-injury notes:			
Signature of coach:			

Goal Planner

(Fill one in for each long-term goal)

Long-term goal:		Weekly Goals												Achieved by
Monthly Goal														

Goal Planner
(Fill one in for each long-term goal)

Performer Profile Form

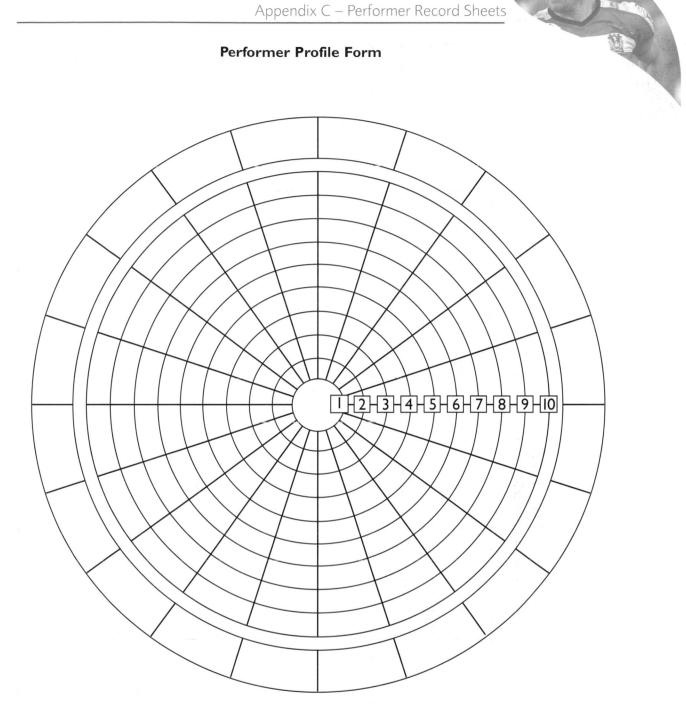